HERBERT
HOOVER

PRESIDENTIAL ✦ LEADERS

HERBERT HOOVER

AMY RUTH

LERNER PUBLICATIONS COMPANY/MINNEAPOLIS

For their friendship and immeasurable kindness, this book is dedicated with love and thanks to Jan and Bill Walker.

The author would like to acknowledge the staff of the Herbert Hoover Presidential Library in West Branch, Iowa, where much of the research for this book was conducted. Special thanks go to archivists Matt Schaefer and Lynn Smith for their invaluable assistance. Because this book was written, in part, during a residency at the Virginia Center for the Creative Arts, the author gratefully acknowledges the VCCA for its unconditional support of individual artists.

Lerner Publications Company
A division of Lerner Publishing Group
241 First Avenue North
Minneapolis, MN 55401 U.S.A.

Website address: www.lernerbooks.com

Library of Congress Cataloging-in-Publication Data

Ruth, Amy.
    Herbert Hoover / by Amy Ruth.
       p.   cm. — (Presidential leaders)
    Includes bibliographical references and index.
    Contents: An Iowa boyhood—Stanford University—The great engineer—The great humanitarian—Just the man—Mr. Prosperity—The presidency—Elder statesman.
    ISBN: 0–8225–0821–4 (lib. bdg. : alk. paper)
    1. Hoover, Herbert, 1874–1964—Juvenile literature. 2. Presidents—United States—Biography—Juvenile literature. [1. Hoover, Herbert, 1874–1964. 2. Presidents.] I. Title. II. Series.
E802.R88 2004
973.91'6'092—dc22   2003022684

Manufactured in the United States of America
1 2 3 4 5 6 – JR – 09 08 07 06 05 04

CONTENTS

———— ✧ ————

Hoover came to be called the Great Humanitarian because of his great efforts to help people around the world.

INTRODUCTION

Democracy is a harsh employer.
—Eugene Lyons,
Hoover biographer

In August 1919, fifty thousand Polish children crowded into an outdoor arena in the city of Warsaw to honor the man who had ensured their survival during years of war. Dressed in rags and waving paper flags, the children marched in formation. A chorus of excited voices rang out in unison as the children chanted, "Long Live Hoover! Long Live Hoover!" Seated on a grandstand, forty-five-year-old Herbert Hoover stayed for hours so that each child could march past and have a glimpse of him.

During World War I (1914–1918), Herbert Hoover organized and put into action a massive relief effort, shipping millions of tons of food every month to citizens living in war-torn and enemy-occupied European countries. Because of Hoover, millions of people in Poland, France, Belgium, and other European countries escaped starvation during and after the war.

Hoover was a successful businessman who was known as much for his cool demeanor as he was for his exceptional organizational skills. Nevertheless, he was visibly moved by the celebration in his honor. A Polish newspaper reported, "The tears are flowing from his good, wise face."

When he was elected the thirty-first president of the United States in 1928, Hoover had been called one of the ten most important people living in the United States. But within months, his reputation as the Great Humanitarian would be disregarded, as the nation (and the world) blamed him for the most severe economic crisis in modern history—the Great Depression.

The anti-Hoover sentiment produced by the Great Depression marred his public image for decades. Hoover was often portrayed as an emotionless aristocrat out of touch with the plight of ordinary people. In reality, he was a caring and sensitive man who had trouble expressing his emotions. He abandoned a brilliant business career that would have made him a fortune to dedicate his life to serving the citizens of the world, never benefiting financially from his work. As a result, Herbert Hoover is perhaps the most misunderstood U.S. president.

CHAPTER ONE

AN IOWA BOYHOOD

There is no imprint upon our minds
so deep as those of early boyhood—
mine are the joys of Iowa.
—Herbert Hoover

Herbert Clark Hoover's story begins in West Branch, Iowa, on the night of August 10, 1874. In a tiny two-room cottage, Jesse Hoover paced anxiously as he awaited his child's birth. Even then, Jesse had big plans for his second son, Herbert, who would be called Bertie or Bert. He is said to have referred to the newborn as "another General Grant," after Ulysses S. Grant, the president of the United States at the time. But when Bert was born late that summer night, Jesse and his wife, Hulda, had no way of knowing that their presidential prediction would come true.

The first six years of Bert's life were happy and carefree. The Hoover family, which included older brother Theodore (Tad) and younger sister Mary (May), lived in the small

Bert (left) *and his brother*
Tad (right) *in about 1877.*
Bert also had a sister, May.
✧ ─────────────────

cottage decorated with Jesse's handcrafted furniture and the rugs Hulda pieced together from rags. Many other members of the Hoover family also lived near West Branch, so visits with aunts, uncles, and cousins were frequent.

Jesse and Hulda had a lot in common. Both were the children of pioneers and came from devout religious families that had belonged to the Society of Friends, or Quakers, for several generations. As members of the Society of Friends, they lived by strong Quaker ideals of peace, service, hard work, and ambition. The family regularly worshiped in quiet meditation in the West Branch Friends Meetinghouse. Even young children like Bert, who found it hard to sit still, had to be quiet and thoughtful during the meetings.

Like other children of the time, Bert, Tad, and May had chores to keep them busy. After a breakfast of cornmeal mush and milk, Bert chopped wood and hauled water to the house from an outside pump. In the springtime, Hulda's garden burst with golden marigolds, red and pink peonies, snapdragons, clusters of phlox, and deep red tulips. Her children helped weed the flower garden and hoe the vegetable patch.

When they finished their chores after school, Tad, Bert, and May were allowed to play. Bert and Tad roamed the woodlands and prairies nearby, pursuing prairie chickens, pigeons, and rabbits. In the summer, the Hoover children enjoyed the swimming hole. In the winter, they grabbed their homemade sleds and headed for snow-covered Cook's Hill. Tad and Bert soared down on their stomachs, their heels high and toes pointed.

Bert and Tad also loved to watch their father shape horseshoes and other metalworks. Jesse Hoover was a hard-working and skilled blacksmith. The ring of his hammer meeting the anvil could be heard throughout the town.

Jesse Hoover (center) *owned and operated this blacksmith shop in West Branch, Iowa. Bert and his brother liked to play at the shop.*

And the glow of the red-hot coals and irons told passersby not to come too close. But once, five-year-old Bert did. Barefooted, he stepped on a piece of hot iron on the floor of his father's shop. Years later, he remarked in his memoirs, "I carry the brand of Iowa on my foot to this day."

The cool waters of Wapsinonoc Creek in West Branch also left a permanent impression on young Bert. As a boy, he fished, using a piece of string as line, a bit of cork as a float, and a pole made from a willow branch. Before slipping the worm onto the hook, Bert spat on it for good luck. The young fisherman caught plenty of sunfish and catfish for the family's dinner table.

Another of Bert's favorite pastimes was walking with his friends along the tracks of the Burlington, Cedar Rapids, and Great Northern Railroad. They spent hours eyeing the ground for pebbles, coral, shells, and fossils. The children enjoyed polishing, showing off, and trading these treasures. Bert especially enjoyed his geological finds. In the West Branch schoolhouse the Hoover children attended, Bert studied the rocks and shells the teacher had on display.

ORPHANS

By the time Bert was five years old, his father was becoming successful in a farm equipment business. He sold the two-room cottage and blacksmith shop, and the Hoovers moved to a larger house one block away. But the Hoover family's happy life came to an end soon after. In December 1880, Jesse Hoover died of a heart attack.

Shortly after his father's death, Bert was sent to Oklahoma for several months. His uncle Laban Miles worked for the U.S. government as an Indian agent on Oklahoma's

Bert was only nine years old when his mother, Hulda (right), died in 1884. Her death orphaned the Hoover children. The Hoover children found places to live with family, but they could not live together.

─────────────── ✧

Osage reservation. During the months away from home, six-year-old Bert learned more and more about the great outdoors. He enjoyed adventuring with his cousins and their Native American friends. From them, he learned many outdoor and survival skills, such as how to build a campfire and how to use a bow and arrow.

Tragedy visited the Hoover children again three years later. A gifted speaker, Hulda Hoover traveled frequently to minister to other Quakers. On her way home from one of these trips, she became ill with typhoid fever and pneumonia. She died in February 1884.

The orphaned Hoover children were separated and sent to live with relatives across Iowa. Seven-year-old May went to live with Hulda's mother, and nine-year-old Bert and thirteen-year-old Tad were sent to live with uncles.

Separated by great distances from his brother and sister, Bert had lost not only his parents but also his siblings.

Bert went to live with his uncle Allan Hoover, his aunt Millie, and his cousin Walter on their farm outside of West Branch. Running a farm was busy and laborious work, and Bert was expected to help. In the summer, Uncle Allan paid Bert and Walter to do farm chores and odd jobs. The boys used their earnings to buy firecrackers for Fourth of July celebrations.

Like his parents, Aunt Millie and Uncle Allan were strict Quakers, and Bert continued his religious learning in their home. "[B]efore I had left Iowa I had read the Bible in daily stints from cover to cover," he remembered years later. Throughout his life, Bert was guided by his Quaker faith. He later remarked that the memory of his mother, who so often was moved to speak during the Friends' meetings, gave him much strength.

THE MINTHORNS

After one year, Dr. Henry John Minthorn, an uncle living in Oregon, wrote to the West Branch relatives. He and his wife had recently lost their only son and suggested that Bert come west to live with them. So at the age of eleven, Bert boarded a train for Oregon. Under the care of a local Quaker family also traveling west, he made the seven-day journey to his new home.

As the train chugged westward, Hoover saw for the first time the rugged terrain of the western landscape. Some geological formations—such as Castle Rock in Colorado and the Devil's Slide in California—enthralled him, but others let him down. "I reported by letter to my teacher, Miss Mollie

Brown, my disappointment that the Rocky Mountains were made mostly of dirt," he wrote in his memoirs.

Bert began his new life in Newberg, a Quaker community in northwestern Oregon, where he lived with the Minthorn family—Uncle John, Aunt Laura, and their three daughters. "I was at once put to school and the chores," Hoover wrote. He milked the cows, chopped wood, and fed his uncle's horses twice a day. Dr. Minthorn frequently traveled throughout the area making house calls to patients, and it was Bert's job to ready the horses for travel. Sometimes Bert accompanied his uncle on these rounds and learned about medicine.

Hoover enrolled at the Friends Pacific Academy, a Quaker school that his uncle directed. Bert was a fair student who had a gift for mathematics, but he was painfully quiet and shy. Burt Barker, a classmate and friend, remembered, "he was . . . a boy of very few words."

Despite his many responsibilities on the Minthorn farm, Bert did find time for fun. He enjoyed baseball and checkers and exploring Oregon's woods and fields. Bert fell in love with the Oregon landscape, and the time he spent there cemented his passion for fishing and his lifelong interest in the outdoors.

Thrift and economy were important Quaker values, and Bert would stick to them all of his life. In Oregon he worked weeding onions one summer. "I returned with some $30," he remembered. "It was a great sum and I kept it or part of it for a long time." He recorded his earnings in a small account book he had brought with him from Iowa.

Although Bert respected the Minthorns a great deal and was grateful to them, he and his uncle often disagreed.

Bert felt his uncle overworked him on the farm and was too strict and sometimes even harsh. Burt Barker remembered that Bert once said that he "felt there was a difference in the way he was treated when his father and mother were alive and the way he was treated as an orphan."

ON HIS OWN

When Bert was fifteen, Uncle John moved his family to nearby Salem, the capital city of Oregon, where he founded a land company with a group of Quaker men. Instead of attending high school, Bert was employed as an office boy in his uncle's company, but running errands did not interest him. Always curious and driven, Bert used his spare time in the office to help the firm's accountant and secretary. From them, he learned the basics of bookkeeping and how to type. At night Bert took classes at a business school.

With a friend, Bert also invested in the repairing and selling of sewing machines. Although the business failed financially, Bert could be proud knowing that he had tried something new in the Quaker spirit of individual enter-prise. He knew that bettering himself and enhancing his skills were necessary for him to become self-sufficient.

The Minthorns were less strict about reading literature, newspapers, and magazines than were some Quakers, and for the first time, Bert could read almost anything he wanted. A local teacher, Jane Gray, took him to the public library and helped him choose books to check out and take home. "That opening of the door to a great imaginative world led me promptly through [many books], often at the cost of sleep," Hoover wrote as an adult. "Suddenly I began to see books as living things and was ready for more of them."

Quakers: The Society of Friends

The Society of Friends religious movement, led by George Fox, began in England in the mid-seventeenth century. Persecuted for their beliefs in England, many Friends, or Quakers, sought a better life in the New World and immigrated to North America.

Quakers emphasize individuality and believe in each person's Inner Light, a moral compass that guides direct communication with God. Quakers worship in a meetinghouse. Their meetings are a time for self-reflection and communication with God. Because Quakers believe every person has a special relationship with God, most Quaker congregations traditionally have not had a religious leader, such as a minister or a priest. When a Friend is moved to speak during a meeting, he or she does so.

Overall, Quakers are concerned with helping others. They believe in equality for all people and oppose war. Instead, they promote justice and peace. During the Civil War, for example, most Quakers refused to fight for either side. They bitterly opposed slavery and often helped escaped slaves by hiding them in their homes or by taking them from one safe house to another on the Underground Railroad. Many Quakers moved out of the South, where most people owned slaves, to the Northwest Territory (present-day upper midwestern United States), where owning slaves was against the law.

Quakers settled West Branch, Iowa, in 1844. Friends—including the Hoovers and the Minthorns—came from Maine, Pennsylvania, Vermont, and Ohio. By the time Herbert was born, West Branch was a prosperous community held together by strong Quaker ideals and values that left a permanent mark on the future president of the United States. As a member of the Quaker faith, Herbert Hoover lived his life according to Quaker principles of thrift, humility, simplicity, helpfulness, individual responsibility, and tolerance.

In Salem, Bert was also reunited with his siblings. May had moved to Salem with Grandmother Minthorn, and Tad was a student at the Quaker Academy in Newberg. For the time being, Jesse and Hulda Hoover's three children had left Iowa and become citizens of the West.

After two years of working as an office boy, Bert was ready to continue his education beyond night school. His relatives wanted him to attend a Quaker college and offered to help him win a scholarship. Bert had other ideas. He wanted to study mechanical engineering. From a Quaker friend, he learned about Stanford University, a new college in California that needed students and did not charge tuition. So when Dr. Joseph Swain, a Stanford representative and a Quaker, came to Oregon to recruit students, Bert eagerly signed on. Although Bert failed all but one of the entrance exams,

✧ ————————————

The Hoover children at about the time of their first reunion during the late 1800s. (From left to right) Tad, May, *and* Bert.

Dr. Swain encouraged him to try again at the end of the summer. He suggested that Bert move to the Stanford area and spend his summer preparing to take the exams a second time.

His fate decided, Bert left for California in June 1891. "The Minthorn family put me on the train with blessings, affections—and food," he later recalled in his memoirs. Nearly seventeen years old, the orphan from Iowa was truly on his own.

CHAPTER TWO

STANFORD UNIVERSITY

Stanford is the best place in the world.
—Herbert Hoover

Hoover spent the summer of 1891 preparing to retake his university entrance exams. He roomed in a boardinghouse run by two schoolteachers. They tutored him, and he took care of their horses. Dr. Swain continued his interest in the Quaker orphan too and took him under his wing that summer. He and his wife assisted Hoover with his studies, and Mrs. Swain sometimes hired him for odd jobs.

After weeks of preparation, Hoover took and passed all but one of the entrance examinations. His performance on the English test was below acceptable standards. He was only permitted to enroll at Stanford with the understanding that before he could graduate, he would have to show a marked improvement in this subject.

Hoover took his place among the first students to attend Stanford University. He began his university career with the same hard work and determination he applied to everything he did.

While there was no charge for tuition at Stanford, students had to pay for their room, board, books, and other expenses. Looking to earn money, Hoover identified the needs of his fellow students and launched some successful enterprises to meet those needs. He ran a laundry service and a concert series and organized a campus paper route. He eventually sold the laundry business to another student for a profit.

STUDYING ROCKS

During Hoover's second term at Stanford, Professor John Branner arrived to head the geology and mines department. Hoover's boyhood interest in rocks and fossils, born along the train tracks of West Branch, was rekindled. Branner was one of the most distinguished geologists of the time.

——————— ✧

At Stanford, John Branner renewed Hoover's curiosity about rocks and fossils. Branner was Stanford's first professor and later became the university's second president.

"Upon Dr. Branner's arrival I came under the spell of a great scientist and a great teacher," Hoover later recalled.

The admiration was mutual. In fact, almost everyone who came to know Hoover at Stanford was impressed with his capacity for work and his talent for organizing and planning projects. Dr. Branner liked Hoover so much that not long after their meeting he hired him as his assistant, a job that gave Hoover a steady income.

"It was characteristic of him that when a task was set before him he took off his coat, fixed his whole attention to the task in hand, and went at it and did it," Branner said of his star pupil. "When something had to be done, he did it whether he liked it or didn't like it; he used his judgement, and he asked only necessary questions. If he made a mistake anywhere along the line, he recognized it, acknowledged it, and said it wouldn't happen again, and it never did."

At semester's end, Branner recommended Hoover to work on a geological survey project. The opportunity took him to Arkansas and the Ozark Mountains, where he spent the summer of 1892 tromping for miles and mapping geological regions. Will Irwin, a Stanford classmate and lifelong friend, remembered that Hoover returned to school in the fall of 1892 "as lean as a greyhound, as hard as nails, and as brown as a berry."

During the following summers, Hoover did similar work for the U.S. Geological Survey in California and Nevada. As he became acquainted with mines, his fascination with mining grew quickly. Around the campfires after dinner, he listened intently as the more experienced members of the team talked shop. Hoover later remembered, "a great amount of engineering lore and practice seeped into my mind."

Hoover (sitting, left) with members of the survey team
he joined while attending Stanford University.

─────────────────── ✧ ───────────────────

Hoover enjoyed his fieldwork tremendously—so much so that one summer, without money to pay for transportation, he walked eighty miles to join a survey team. Returning home to begin his senior year after a summer of surveying, he wrote to a friend, "Learned much and am better morally, physically & financially than 6 months ago."

REORGANIZING STANFORD

At Stanford, Hoover first showed his greatest talents: the ability to successfully orchestrate large and complicated projects and a keen knack for problem solving. He brought these talents to bear on the student body, because the dismal state of student-run organizations bothered him greatly.

To make the changes he thought were needed, Hoover, then in his third year, organized some of his friends to run for student government. With a fresh slate of new officers and Hoover as student body treasurer, reform could begin. He introduced a new student body constitution and put into effect systems and procedures that greatly improved how student clubs and student government were managed.

In particular, it bothered Hoover that there seemed to be no accountability for student body finances, which were in terrible condition. During his junior year (1893–1894), Hoover published the student body's financial records in the student newspaper. He also reorganized the junior class finances and paid off its three-year-old debt of two thousand dollars.

Hoover even successfully managed the school's baseball and football teams, doing everything from scheduling games to securing equipment. And he put his problem-solving skills to work for the student-run store, which was also failing financially before Hoover stepped in. One classmate remarked on Hoover's efficient and earnest manner, saying that Hoover "always ignored the unessentials and got to the heart of any situation."

LOU HENRY

Despite his many outgoing and aggressive campus projects, Hoover was a shy young man who found it difficult to express his feelings. He often came across as cool and distant. One student described him as having "hazel eyes so contemplative that they seemed dreamy." Hoover's shyness

TREASURER HOOVER'S REPORT

Of the Football Season From a Financial Standpoint. The Season Not so Successful as Many Supposed.

With this issue we begin the publication of the report of Treasurer Hoover to the Executive Committee. This report contains the reports of the treasurer, football, baseball, and track managers up to date. A general summary will be given later, in which the expenditures and receipts of the present season are compared in detail with those of last year.

This is the first year that the financial affairs have been thrown open to the Student Body; and with this year a precedent is established that must be followed in the future.

In giving expenditures it is impossible to publish minute details, as such would fill a volume, but items are segregated so as to give as clear an idea as possible. Treasurer Hoover's voucher books and detailed statements are open to all those who care to take the trouble to look over them.

GENERAL SUMMARY.

RECEIPTS.		DR.	CR.
(1) By Football season	$6620	41	
(2) " Annual assessment	431	00	
(3) " Trustees for track	30	00	
(4) " Lecture for track by Dr Jordan	66	25	
(5) " Borrowed money	385	00	
(6) " Ex-Treas Chase	4	15	

EXPENDITURES.			
(1) To Football season			$5824 73
(2) " Track management			400 25
(3) " Baseball management			150 00
(4) " Old debts discharged			468 01
(5) " Borrowed money returned			385 00
(6) " Incidentals			35 40

Part of the financial report Hoover wrote as student body treasurer during his junior year (1893–1894)

─────── ✧ ───────

made it difficult for his fellow students to get to know him, but they generally respected him.

By Hoover's own admission, his interest at Stanford centered on his extracurricular activities rather than on academics, in which he was usually average. But it was during his senior year that he discovered yet another interest—Miss Lou Henry, Stanford University's first female geology student.

Hoover later described their first meeting in Dr. Branner's geology laboratory as "a major event in my life." As an upperclassman and an accomplished lab assistant, Hoover took it upon himself to orient Lou to her new surroundings. "I felt it my duty to aid the young lady in her studies, both in the laboratory and in the field,"

———————————————— ✧ ————————————————

Lou Henry at the time she attended Stanford University. She was the first female geology student to attend Stanford. Hoover liked Lou's smile.

Hoover wrote. "And this call to duty was stimulated by her whimsical mind, her blue eyes, and a broad grinnish smile. . . ."

It was said that Lou could make almost anyone feel comfortable, and indeed, Hoover's shyness seemed to slip away in her company. In addition to their geology coursework, Lou and Hoover shared a great love of the outdoors, and the two quickly became good friends.

LIFE AFTER STANFORD

Hoover's hard work and entrepreneurial spirit allowed him to graduate from Stanford University in 1895 with no debts and forty dollars in his pocket. That summer he again joined a U.S. Geological Survey team, charting territory in Nevada and California. Hoover had hoped that this summer work would turn into a full-time position, but cuts in government funding ended the project.

Hoover had trouble finding work and eventually was forced to take a low-paying job pushing carts deep underground in the mine shafts of California. The work was hard and repetitive, and his seven-day workweek kept him in the mines ten hours at a time. Although Hoover did not enjoy the difficult, monotonous work, he was grateful to have a job at all in what were tough economic times in the United States. In addition, he knew that he was learning about the mining field from the bottom up and that what he was learning would surely be useful to him in the future. He was pleased when the other miners accepted him as one of their own, and he became, in his words, a "real miner."

In 1896 he left his job in the mines, hoping to find a position in the office of a mining engineer in San Francisco.

Again unable to find work as a mining engineer, he took a job as an office boy in a mining firm. The firm was run by the successful and internationally known Louis Janin. Hoover was certain that if given the opportunity, he could show Janin how useful and capable he was. That opportunity presented itself when Janin's firm was helping with a lawsuit between two mining companies. The work required the preparation and collection of a lot of technical data, much of which was done by Hoover. With the successful resolution of the lawsuit came new prospects for Hoover. Before long, Janin had him evaluating new mines as a mine scout.

Life was good for Hoover, not only professionally but also personally. Living in San Francisco, he could court Lou Henry, who was still a student at nearby Stanford. And for the first time since childhood, the three children of Jesse

Lou Henry graduated from Stanford in 1898. Hoover's brother, Theodore, also attended the university.

and Hulda Hoover were living together under the same roof. Tad worked as a pressman for a newspaper, and May was in high school. Theodore had been taking engineering classes at Stanford, but after the death of Grandmother Minthorn, he dropped out of school to look after his sister. Hoover hoped that if he could find a better paying job, his brother could quit his job and return to Stanford.

Things just seemed to get better and better for Bert Hoover. When the English firm of Bewick, Moreing and Company asked Janin to recommend a person to manage the company's mining interests in Australia, Janin's choice was twenty-two-year-old Hoover.

CHAPTER THREE

THE GREAT ENGINEER

*My . . . ambition was to be able to earn my
own living, without the help of anybody,
anywhere.*

—Herbert Hoover

When Bert Hoover presented himself to the London executives of Bewick, Moreing and Company, he was at the beginning of what would become a distinguished international career. To look older and more experienced, he had grown a mustache. Despite his shy and quiet ways, Hoover impressed his new boss Charles Moreing.

Hoover arrived in Australia at the height of that country's gold rush. He made his new home in the remote western regions of Coolgardie and Kalgoorlie, where gold had only recently been discovered. The region was hot, dry, and dusty, receiving barely more than one inch of rain a year. There were no streams for fishing or bathing. "[I]t's a country of red dust, black flies and white heat," Hoover wrote

At twenty-three, Hoover grew a mustache to impress his new bosses at Bewick, Moreing and Company. They were expecting someone at least thirty-five years old.
─────── ✧

to a friend in Oregon. "The country is an endless desert, no water, no nothing but mines." But there was gold—and plenty of it.

Once he arrived in the Coolgardie mining camp, Hoover put to use his immense ability to plan, organize, and troubleshoot. From his previous U.S. mining experience and Quaker upbringing, he had developed an intense, if not unwelcome, belief in the superiority of U.S. mining techniques. He brought in U.S. equipment and introduced what were considered new and innovative mining methods. Water was scarce, so water conservation was essential to the success of the company's mining efforts. Hoover showed the mine managers and workers how to filter and reuse water. Later, he served on a committee of mine operators that convinced the Australian government to pipe in water to the remote and dusty region.

Members of Hoover's mining team riding camels. Hoover often rode camels to get to mines located in the desert of Australia's interior.

———————————— ✧ ————————————

When Hoover wasn't occupied at Coolgardie or Kalgoorlie, he traveled hundreds of miles into the interior of the region to inspect mines that his company might purchase. He often rode on a camel or horseback and camped along the way. The conditions made for hard living and a life without regular showers, fresh fruit, and other comforts.

One mine was of particular interest to Hoover. After much studying, analyzing, and evaluating, he suggested to his superiors at Bewick, Moreing and Company that the company purchase the Sons of Gwalia mine. Hoover's evaluation of the mine resulted in massive profits for the next fifty years. Hoover was promptly rewarded with a salary of $12,500 a year. Hoover became the firm's "chief field engineer," overseeing eight mines in Kalgoorlie. He was quickly named manager of the successful Sons of Gwalia mine. Around this time, he received the nickname Chief, which followed him wherever he worked.

A NEW JOB, A NEW BRIDE

Although Hoover later wrote that he and his staff enjoyed "every hour" of their rugged work, the conditions did begin to wear on him. Anxious to make progress in both his professional and personal life, Hoover was overjoyed when Charles Moreing suggested a transfer to oversee the company's mining interests in China. The new job doubled his salary. "[N]ever was a message more enthusiastically received," Hoover remembered years later.

After sending a telegram to Charles Moreing accepting the job, he sent another one to Lou Henry, his former Stanford classmate. She had graduated from Stanford and was teaching school in California. Hoover asked Lou to marry him. Her answer was yes.

Lou Henry and Herbert Hoover were married on February 10, 1899, in the Henry home in Monterey, California. Although Lou had decided to become a Quaker, no Quaker meetinghouse was close by, so a Catholic priest and friend of the family married the couple. A wedding portrait of the Hoovers shows a clean-shaven Bert. Gone was the mustache that just a year before he thought he needed to impress others.

The newlyweds set sail almost immediately for their new home in northern China. The long journey provided plenty of time to read about the Chinese people and culture. Once there they lived temporarily in Peking (Beijing) before moving to the port city of Tientsin (Tianjin). They rented a house in a section of Tientsin where other foreign families lived clustered together.

Mrs. Hoover began daily Chinese language lessons. "With a natural gift for languages she made great progress in the most difficult tongue in the world," Hoover remembered. "I never absorbed more than a hundred words."

————————————— ✧ —————————————

Lou Henry (left center) and Hoover (bottom) with members of the Henry family on their wedding day. Soon after their marriage, the couple set sail for China.

THE GREAT FOREIGN MANDARIN

Charles Moreing had several reasons for selecting Hoover to oversee the company's mining operations in China. Hoover had proved himself very capable both in the field and as a manager. The company also thought that, as a U.S. citizen, he might be better received in a country where European people and influences were becoming less tolerated. In his new position, Hoover was to find and develop mines in China and to set up resources that supported the mining industry—from a reliable system of railroad tracks to a good port in northern China. At the same time, Hoover served as an adviser to the Chinese, working in the newly created Ministry of Mines.

When Hoover arrived at the first mine site he was to inspect in China, he was surprised by the throngs of people waiting for him. Hoover's reputation as a talented mining engineer had preceded him. "[W]ord had been sent ahead that a great foreign mandarin [a high official] was coming who could see through the ground and find gold," Hoover said.

THE BOXER REBELLION

Despite the warm welcome the Hoovers received, the growing presence of foreigners and foreign influences infuriated a large group of Chinese who feared the outsiders would take over China. In the summer of 1900, a group that called itself the "Righteous and Harmonious Fists" swept through parts of China, killing foreigners and Chinese Christians and burning churches. The Boxers, as the secret society became known, neared Tientsin in June. The Hoovers and other foreigners thought they would be safe because they were protected by Chinese troops allied with them.

Chinese soldiers defend Tientsin from advancing Boxer rebels. Many Chinese soldiers switched sides during the rebellion, joining the Boxers.

———————————— ✧ ————————————

When the Boxers swarmed into the city, however, many of the Chinese soldiers rushed to join them as they attacked the foreign residential district.

A small delegation of foreign relief troops was all that was left to defend against the siege. To hold off the attackers, the residents themselves sprung into action, with twenty-six-year-old Hoover in the lead. Hoover and other men organized the residents to build barricades using sacks of sugar, rice, peanuts, and grain that were stored in city warehouses.

In addition to the foreign residents, hundreds of Chinese citizens who did not support the Boxers had fled their homes to take refuge in the foreign part of Tientsin. Hoover again sprung into action—securing and distributing food, water, and other necessary items for these people.

He also helped extinguish the many fires caused by the shooting and shelling and was one of several men who crept out of the barricades at night to fetch water. During one incident, Hoover saved a little Chinese girl, carrying her out of her burning home to safety.

The Hoovers worked tirelessly during the monthlong siege, often putting themselves at risk. Both took turns guarding the city's boundaries, and Lou even carried a gun. The city was under constant attack. The Boxers, who numbered in the tens of thousands, had surrounded the foreign section. About three hundred people were killed inside the city, and many more were injured. Lou spent most of her time helping care for the wounded in the city's hospitals.

———————————————— ✧ ————————————————

Lou Henry Hoover stands with one of the cannons the Europeans used to hold off Boxer rebels at Tientsin, China.

Several Stanford graduates were known to be living and working in Tientsin, so newspapers in California followed the rebellion closely. One newspaper, thinking the Hoovers had died, even printed Lou's obituary.

Of his wife's activities during the siege, Hoover recalled "I saw little of her . . . except when she came home occasionally to eat or catch a little sleep. She became expert in riding her bicycle close to the walls of buildings to avoid stray bullets and shells."

In July more fighting troops, including U.S. Marines, arrived in Tientsin, and the Boxers were driven away. Exhausted and relieved, the Hoovers did not stop their good work. With the military reinforcements came foreign officers and journalists. The Hoovers opened their home and their work to all of them, giving them what little hospitality they could manage.

MORE CHANGES AHEAD

A month after the siege ended, the Hoovers prepared for a trip to London. Before leaving, Hoover was presented with a business opportunity that would benefit Bewick, Moreing and Company and prevent a competitor from seizing the valuable Chinese mining company. A deal was struck with the Chinese, and control of the threatened company was transferred to Bewick, Moreing and Company. Hoover's superiors appointed Hoover general manager of the new endeavor.

After stopping in the United States, the Hoovers returned to China. Trouble bubbled up quickly in Hoover's new company, however. A group representing a Belgian business had purchased enough stock to win control and had even named a new manager to replace Hoover.

Furious and frustrated, Hoover prepared to quit his job. Although he was only twenty-seven years old, Hoover had gained a wealth of experience and knowledge and was quickly becoming a well-known and respected engineer. He knew he would continue to advance his career, whether he remained with Bewick, Moreing and Company or returned to California in search of new opportunities. The thought of losing such a valuable employee prompted Bewick, Moreing and Company to offer Hoover a partnership in the firm, with stock options and part ownership. Best of all, the position meant relocating to London.

CHAPTER FOUR

THE GREAT HUMANITARIAN

I did not realize it at the moment but . . . my
engineering career was over forever. I was on
the slippery road of public life.
—Herbert Hoover

As a junior partner with Bewick, Moreing and Company, Hoover had a significant presence in the mining and financial worlds. One newspaper, in reporting his new position, remarked that Hoover was "the highest salaried man of his age in the world." Not yet thirty years old, Hoover was earning about thirty-three thousand dollars a year, a huge amount of money at that time. In addition to his salary, money came from company stocks and other personal investments and mining projects.

Hoover's work required him to be away from home frequently, often for weeks at a time. From time to time, his family accompanied him. The Hoovers' first son, Herbert Jr., was born in 1903, and only weeks after his birth, both he and his mother joined Hoover on a business trip to Australia. Between 1901 and 1908, Hoover's business travels took him all over the world.

THE RED HOUSE
In 1907 the Hoover family grew again. A second son, Allan, was born in August of that year, and the Hoovers moved to a larger London residence, a brick house that they came to call the Red House. Family life in the Red House was relaxed and fun, and the Hoovers entertained dinner guests almost every night. The Hoovers were happy living in London, although their modest, unassuming ways often clashed with British high society.

THE HIGHE/T /ALARIED MAN OF HIS AGE IN THE WORLD

Salaried Man of Age in the World.

HERBERT C. HOO-VER, a young

Ten years ago Hoover entered Stanford University a poor boy. He had to work for the money that paid his modest expenses at college. He was a hard student. Men and women who were at Stanford those first four years of the young university's life will recall Hoover as a quiet young fellow who was habitually deep in some treatise or close over some fossil specimen, or profile

Hoover became a partner in Bewick, Moreing and Company in 1901, making him one of the highest paid men in the world.

Lou Hoover (center) *with the Hoover sons, Allan* (left) *and Bert Jr.* (right). *In addition to raising the boys, Lou often worked with Hoover on his papers about geology and mining.*

✧ ——————————

Even though they had lived for some time in England, the Hoovers were patriotic U.S. citizens who wanted their children to have a U.S.-based upbringing and education. As the boys grew, the Hoovers also instilled in them the simple Quaker values of modesty, thrift, and individual enterprise. Hoover took great pleasure in his children and wanted a happy childhood for his sons. "Cheerless homes produce morbid minds," he once remarked. A newspaper reporter wrote of the Hoover household, "Malice, envy, clamor, wrath and hatred, in act or word, are singularly absent from the Hoovers' way of life."

Hoover introduced Allan and Bert Jr. to mining techniques and engineering principles when they were still quite young. On picnics with family and friends, he would demonstrate for the children how to build a dam in a nearby creek or stream. One U.S. visitor to the Red House remembered that when she first met Hoover, he was on the back patio with his sons, panning for gold in the garden fountain.

THE HOOVER TEAM

Hoover firmly believed in the responsible use of U.S. technology. Wherever he traveled, he sought to eliminate waste in production and labor by introducing and implementing U.S. equipment and techniques. His eye for efficiency even helped to improve conditions for workers. Hoover believed that underpaid workers who were forced to work long hours in difficult and dangerous conditions actually cost a company more money.

He wrote extensively about his theories, and his articles appeared frequently in the leading industry periodicals. The once reluctant and struggling student of English composition and grammar was successfully using the written word to reach a respectful and interested audience.

Meanwhile, Hoover and Lou never stopped learning. In 1907 they undertook a massive translation project that would make a significant contribution to geology, mining, and related fields. The Hoovers were fascinated with a sixteenth-century book called *De Re Metallica,* which had to do with mining and the science of metals. An important work, sometimes called "the bible of mining," it had not been successfully or fully translated from its original Latin because so much of the meaning would be lost in the translation.

The Hoovers' attempt was successful because together they had the critical combination of skills—Lou's understanding of Latin, Hoover's mining background, and their mutual knowledge of geology. The translation project would take them five years to complete, but it was published to much acclaim.

DOCTOR OF SICK MINES

With Lou at his side, Hoover spent the first decade of the new century amassing a personal fortune. In 1908 he left the firm of Bewick, Moreing and Company so that he and his family could spend more time in the United States. He began his own mining firm and for the next six years consulted on mining projects worldwide.

Hoover still traveled extensively—he had offices in New York, San Francisco, London, Paris, and Petrograd, Russia—but Lou and the boys lived in California much of the year. The family was reunited in London and spent time in the English countryside during the summers and on school holidays. While they were separated, the Hoovers stayed in touch by letters and telegrams, like the ones Lou sent to her husband one spring: "Herbert Allan Mummy white rabbits white baby chickens toads frogs lizards salamanders horned toad all well and send love" and "both boys caught a string of trout."

Hoover's reputation was just as impressive as his wealth. He was known throughout the industry as a "doctor of sick mines." Engineering companies and mine owners the world over looked to Hoover to make their failing enterprises profitable. He was regarded as a man who got things done, no matter what, and was a valuable addition to any enterprise. In 1912 he was elected to Stanford's board of trustees.

Hoover was so good at saving failing mining operations that people came to call him the doctor of sick mines.

——————————✧

THE SLIPPERY ROAD OF PUBLIC LIFE

Hoover's reputation for efficiency and problem solving prompted the U.S. ambassador to Great Britain to call him the afternoon of August 3, 1914. War had erupted in Europe, following the assassination of Archduke Francis Ferdinand by a Serbian patriot acting on his own. Within a week, thousands of U.S. travelers throughout Europe scrambled toward London and away from the progressing war. The onset of war destabilized European economies, and tens of thousands of U.S. tourists suddenly found themselves unable to cash their travelers checks or conduct other business. Without money, the tourists could not pay for hotel rooms, meals, or transportation home. In desperation, they arrived at the U.S. consulate in London. It was the height of the tourist season.

Throngs of panicked and exhausted U.S. citizens quickly filled the city.

The Hoovers had been about to return to California, but there was no question that they would stay in London and do whatever they could to help their fellow U.S. citizens. And so began Hoover's fifty-year career in public service. Looking back on this time in London, Hoover later remarked, "I did not realize it at the moment but . . . my engineering career was over forever. I was on the slippery road of public life."

Hoover immediately responded to the U.S. ambassador's plea for help. In a few days, Hoover had gathered together friends, associates, and fellow engineers to organize the American Citizens' Relief Committee in the ballroom of London's Savoy Hotel. One of Hoover's strengths was his ability to mobilize people to action. Within days, U.S. citizens and corporations were extending financial support to the committee. The U.S. government shipped a cargo of currency to the group, and about 500 people volunteered to help. In six weeks, the committee assisted 120,000 troubled U.S. citizens and extended $1.5 million in loans. The borrowers repaid all but $300 of that money.

While her husband tended to the financial needs of the stranded tourists, Lou Hoover addressed the specific concerns of women and children. She set up the Women's Committee and collected clothing, blankets, and other personal items. She was a reassuring and calming force during a frantic time.

THE CRB

While the Hoovers were aiding stranded tourists, German soldiers were invading Belgium. German soldiers occupied the nation. They ransacked the small, highly populated country. Entire towns were destroyed, and railroads and telegraph lines were paralyzed.

Even worse, Belgium produced only 20 percent of its food. The other 80 percent was imported. But German soldiers controlled travel and shipping in and out of the country. They took crops, cattle, and other foodstuffs from the Belgians to feed the German army. Belgium was quickly becoming a nation of ten million starving people.

————————————— ✧ —————————————

Starving Belgian children hold out bowls for food rations during World War I. Hoover was asked to organize a group to help feed European children during the war.

In October 1914, European and U.S. diplomats appealed to Hoover to undertake a massive relief effort to prevent widespread famine in Belgium. Such a project would require nothing less than Hoover's full attention. That meant an end, at least temporarily, to his profitable business career, which by 1914 had brought him a personal fortune of several million dollars. Leading the relief effort also meant that he would be separated for months at a time from his family, who had already returned to California.

After reorganizing and shifting responsibilities for his company and personal business interests, Hoover accepted the task of organizing the relief effort. He insisted, however, that two conditions be met. The first, Hoover told the Belgian ambassador, was that he would accept no salary. The second condition was that he be given "absolute command" of the initiative.

Hoover—along with businessmen such as Emile Francqui, Julius H. Barnes, Prentiss Gray, Edgar Rickard, and John Lowery Simpson—formed the Commission for Relief in Belgium (CRB). The commission began work immediately. For the next three years, Hoover immersed himself in the work of the CRB. The task was enormous, and the stakes were high. Representatives of the CRB had been asked to do something that had never been attempted before. The fate of a nation rested with their efforts. The details and politics of running the CRB against the backdrop of a world war posed great challenges.

The CRB's task dealt with the purchase, transportation, and distribution of massive amounts of food—enough to feed ten million people every day. Hoover appealed to the world for the money needed to buy food and pay transportation costs. He applied for and received government grants. He organized U.S. volunteers in Belgium to set up and run food distribution centers.

Within the first weeks of the CRB effort, Hoover came to realize that he had underestimated the scope of the task. Initially, Hoover thought the CRB would need to raise one million dollars and ship around twenty thousand tons of food to Belgium each month. Hoover quickly discovered that the commission would need to raise about five million dollars every month and make monthly shipments of eighty thousand tons of food, and these numbers rose steadily.

In ordinary circumstances the CRB's job would have been daunting. In the middle of a war, the work was frustrating, risky, and seemingly against all odds. Hoover remarked, "Throughout the Relief it was difficult to determine which were our worst troubles—governments, food, finance, or ships."

Other problems were those of politics and diplomacy. Because the CRB was organized as a politically neutral organization, the German government reluctantly agreed to let CRB representatives and supplies into Belgium. Nevertheless, CRB ships were sometimes attacked at sea, and tons of food were destroyed.

Some politicians argued that feeding the citizens of occupied Belgium was the same as helping the enemy. German soldiers often stole the food and supplies meant for the Belgians. Hoover argued that starving people did not have the luxury of waiting for politicians to end their bickering. CRB representatives were also accused of spying for the enemy. A U.S. senator even accused Hoover of spying for Germany and demanded that he be brought to trial.

Hoover ignored these accusations and pushed ahead. His actions were precise, efficient, and swift. "He eats, sleeps, lives, almost mechanically, and yet his mind is no mere machine," Smith remembered. "There is something almost terribly personal about it, in its desire that things shall change, that order shall be brought out of an existing chaos."

Hoover worked as many as eighteen hours a day, and one colleague remarked that he never seemed to tire. He ran the CRB with his eye always on the single purpose of

———————————— ✧ ————————————

Cooks prepare meals at a hunger-relief kitchen in Belgium during World War I. The kitchen and its goods were supplied by Hoover's CRB.

saving lives. The work had to be done quickly and effi-
ciently because each shipload of food lasted only a short
time, if it arrived at its destination at all. Hoover rarely
held meetings, which he considered a waste of time.
Instead, he gathered his department heads to brief him over
a working lunch.

Robertson Smith, a CRB colleague, remembered that
"Mr. Hoover dictates his memoranda standing or walking
with his hands in his pockets, jingling his change, concern
written upon his face. He dictates rapidly... using two
men-stenographers, one relieving the other."

Hoover hired auditors from an accounting firm to monitor
the CRB's financial and administrative activities. So efficient
was his administration of the relief effort that the final audi-
tor's report showed that less than 1 percent of all the funds
had been used for the administration of the project. It was
considered remarkable that such a large organization spent
such a small amount of money to get its work done.

In just under three years, the CRB had spent one billion dollars, had purchased and transported five million
tons of food, and had fed more than ten million hungry
people in Belgium, northern France, and Poland. So significant were the accomplishments of the CRB that it was discovered, after the war, that the mortality rate of children
was lower than ever before in Belgian and French history.

Like her husband, Lou Henry Hoover felt the call of
public service. While the Hoover boys attended school in
California, Lou returned to London to assist with war relief
efforts. In London she was instrumental in the American
Woman's Hospital, run entirely by volunteers, which treated
thousands of wounded British soldiers throughout the war.

THE GREAT HUMANITARIAN

By 1917 Hoover was celebrated the world over for his immense humanitarian acts. Walter Hines Page, the U.S. ambassador to Britain, described Hoover as a "[s]imple, modest, energetic...man who began his career in California and will end it in Heaven."

At a dinner held to honor Hoover, his geology professor at Stanford, John Branner, reflected on his former student's success and motivation as a humanitarian. "I do not doubt that one of the reasons he has been so successful in looking after the hungry millions of Europe is that he is a man of

In 1917 President Woodrow Wilson asks the U.S. Congress to approve a declaration of war, bringing the United States into World War I (1914–1918).

broad and deep human sympathies," Dr. Branner told the audience. "No one is touched more quickly or more profoundly by human suffering, and no one is more indignant than he at any injustice done the poor, the weak, and the helpless."

Meanwhile, after years of watching the war in Europe from the outside, the United States became involved. In 1917, President Woodrow Wilson asked Congress to declare war, a move that brought great change to the United States. The nation had to produce and manage enough food to support its army overseas and U.S. citizens at home. It also shipped goods to Allied soldiers and citizens. This challenge called for a person with unique abilities. The Great Humanitarian was the perfect person for the job. At President Woodrow Wilson's request, Hoover returned to the United States to serve as the nation's first food administrator.

CHAPTER FIVE

JUST THE MAN

*Progress must come from individual initiative;
and in time of stress it must be mobilized
through cooperative action.*

—Herbert Hoover, giving an address to the
Chamber of Commerce of the United States

After his tremendous success feeding people in Belgium and
other European nations, Hoover and some of his CRB associates set about organizing the U.S. food supply in the
spring of 1917. The world had responded in full force to
the work of the CRB. Hoover believed the same voluntary
cooperation could be called upon to increase production
and encourage conservation of food in the United States.

In the newly created U.S. Food Administration, Hoover
ran a program that equated food conservation with patrio-
tism. Slogans such as "Food Will Win the War" and "Meatless
Mondays" encouraged families to do their part in conserving food and supporting U.S. troops at war.

In speeches and articles, Hoover appealed directly to those who most often prepared family meals: wives and mothers. In October 1917, he told readers of the *Ladies Home Journal* magazine, "You are a great army drafted by conscience into what is now the most urgent activity of war—that of increasing and conserving the food supply."

Under Hoover's leadership, the United States reduced its food intake by 15 percent in three years. Hoover was particularly proud that the U.S. public did conserve food voluntarily and that no government regulations, or laws, had been required.

──────────────── ✧ ────────────────

A 1917 sign with Hoover slogans urges the conservation of food.

Hang this where you will see it every day.

United States Food Administration

REMEMBER THE DAYS

SUNDAY ..... —One meal Wheatless; one meal Meatless.
MONDAY .... —All meals Wheatless; one meal Meatless.
TUESDAY .... —All meals Meatless; one meal Wheatless.
WEDNESDAY—All meals Wheatless; one meal Meatless.
THURSDAY .. —One meal Wheatless; one meal Meatless.
FRIDAY ...... — One meal Wheatless; one meal Meatless.
SATURDAY .. —All meals Porkless; one meal Wheatless;
                    one meal Meatless.

Food Commissioner Hoover (second from left) at a lunch meeting with European officials. Following World War I, Hoover continued the work he started with the CRB as head of the American Relief Administration.

When World War I ended in 1918, President Wilson asked Hoover to return to Europe to evaluate its food needs. With Hoover at the helm, the postwar American Relief Administration (ARA) supplied food to hungry people in twenty-one countries until 1921.

But food relief was just one area of work for Hoover. Throughout his life, Hoover worked for and advocated world peace. While abroad with the ARA, Hoover founded what would later be called the Hoover Institution on War, Revolution and Peace, located at Stanford University. He created the institution as a way to study the consequences of war and arranged for the collection and processing of thousands of documents from World War I.

Hoover's activities had made him an international hero. Many nations tried to honor the man who had done so much for the citizens of Europe. But ever modest, Hoover refused almost every honor and decoration. In 1922 he did accept a gift from the people of Belgium, who honored him with a bronze statue of Isis, the Egyptian goddess of life. The statue still stands in West Branch, Iowa, not far from Hoover's birthplace. By the time the Hoovers returned home in 1921, Hoover was just as popular in the United States as he was in Europe, and he was quickly sought after as a speaker and consultant.

——————————— ✧ ———————————

Hoover (right center) *stands with a plaque and bags of mail honoring and thanking him for his food relief work in Europe. The two European girls with Hoover presented him with the plaque and letters.*

SECRETARY OF COMMERCE

Although Hoover resumed his mining business and even began building a home near Stanford University, he did not remain out of public life for very long. Some people wanted Hoover to run for president. Instead, he accepted President Warren G. Harding's appointment as secretary of commerce in 1921. He would agree to serve, he said, as long as the president gave him his word to include him in important discussions and decisions in all matters relating to commerce. This request greatly bothered many members of Harding's administration. It seemed to them that Hoover wanted to be secretary of commerce and "under-secretary of all other departments." Hoover quickly became an important adviser to the president, who sought and valued his opinion on many matters of state, even those outside the Commerce Department.

In previous administrations, the Department of Commerce and its secretary wielded little influence and made few contributions to U.S. trade. Hoover meant to change that. He pledged to transform the Department of Commerce into a high-performing arm of the government—an agency that would offer service, support, and assistance to U.S. businesses and industries.

When Hoover took his new job, he found a poorly organized collection of bureaus, each functioning independently. Before the department could improve business and the economy, Hoover had to rid the agency of its own inefficiencies that prevented growth. He promptly reorganized the agency and replaced bureau heads with people whose vision mirrored his. Even the office space of the department—spread out among fifteen buildings—was inefficient. Hoover

Hoover (left) *and Lou* (second from left) *with President Harding* (center). *Harding appointed Hoover as secretary of commerce in 1921.*

began to develop plans for a massive new building that would house all the bureaus of the commerce department.

Meanwhile, the U.S. economy was undergoing problems of its own. The U.S. government had encouraged farmers and manufacturers to produce crops and goods to support wartime needs. But these demands ended after World War I and caused an economic slump. Hoover believed that his plans for the Department of Commerce would lift the nation out of its economic recession. Two weeks after taking office, he told a group of business leaders that the fate of the economy depended on the initiative and cooperation of everyone in the United States—from individuals to entire industries.

Despite the opinions of some colleagues, Hoover believed he could make significant contributions to advance trade and boost the economy. In his eight years as secretary of commerce, he also fought to sharply reduce wastefulness, develop underutilized resources, and standardize industries.

HOOVER'S AMERICAN INDIVIDUALISM

Herbert Hoover's ideal society was based on ordered freedom, which he called American individualism. His ideal had its roots in Quaker values—particularly the principles of individual enterprise, social responsibility, and an unwavering faith in cooperative unity. Hoover also believed strongly in the superiority of U.S. ideas, industriousness, and products.

Hoover's idea of individualism relied on the belief of equal opportunity for everyone. Hoover believed that, given the opportunity, anyone—including a penniless orphan from Iowa—could succeed if he or she worked hard enough. "Each individual shall be given the chance and stimulation for development of the best with which he has been endowed in heart and mind," he wrote.

In 1922 Hoover published his ideas in a book called *American Individualism.* In it he outlined how the principles of his theory could build a better United States and promote world peace. He had seen voluntary cooperation succeed at the highest levels. During his time with the Commission for the Relief of Belgium, millions of Europeans were saved from starvation by the goodwill of others. His enormously successful national food program in the United States was also based on voluntary participation.

———————————————— ✧

Hoover makes the first intercity television broadcast in 1922. Hoover believed in the superiority of U.S. ideas, such as those that led to the invention of television.

During Hoover's years as secretary of commerce, he improved the gathering and sharing of information about U.S. businesses. He also worked with manufacturers to standardize products made by factories. Under Hoover's guidance, factories began making parts and products, such as car wheels and light bulbs, that could be used universally. Before, for example, only a certain light bulb would fit a certain lamp. After the standardization process, any size light bulb made by any manufacturer would fit all sizes of sockets. In turn, the sockets were made to fit the standardized light bulb. Standardization made products safer to use and eliminated waste in production.

In addition, Hoover took over and created other commerce bureaus in order to improve trade with foreign countries. He also regulated radio and airwaves, and promoted safety on U.S. roads and in the sky. In the 1920s, air travel was new and unregulated. Hoover created safety standards, including lights on runways. He also improved and expanded airmail service and wrote highway safety codes and zoning laws.

A WELL-LIVED QUAKER LIFE

Home life for the Hoovers during the commerce years was relaxed and warm, not unlike the many happy times spent in the Red House in London. From his home office, Hoover could walk into the large garden and enjoy a small bit of the outdoors. His important work in the Department of Commerce left little time for fishing and other outdoor pursuits, but Hoover did spend time with his sons. Herbert Jr. and Allan were growing into young men. After high school, both boys followed in their parents' footsteps and attended Stanford University.

Meanwhile, Hoover continued to pursue interests outside the normal role of commerce secretary. To improve the quality of life for everyone, Hoover created Better Homes in America. The project encouraged and made it easier for people to buy homes. To better the environment, Hoover expanded the role of the Bureau of Fisheries to increase fish exports and conserve parks and natural areas.

In 1923 President Harding died unexpectedly, and his vice president, Calvin Coolidge, became the next U.S. president. Hoover continued to serve in Coolidge's cabinet throughout his presidency.

In 1927 Hoover's ability as an organizer was gravely needed in the southern United States. A great flood along the Mississippi River had devastated homes, businesses, crops, and livestock and had left more than half a million people homeless. President Coolidge asked Hoover to take control of the situation. Hoover immediately left for Memphis, Tennessee, where he directed the relief efforts from temporary headquarters set up on river steamboats.

Hoover spent three months on the scene, living in a hot and cramped railroad car, separated from his family. So strong was his belief in public service that he was willing to sacrifice his own comfort for the benefit of others.

The public followed Hoover's activities almost daily in newspaper articles about the successful relief efforts. Hoover credited its success to the voluntary cooperation of citizens and organizations, such as the Red Cross, that stepped in with the needed assistance and funding. Hoover believed that in times of disaster, U.S. citizens should—and would—help each other. The Mississippi relief effort, like all of Hoover's public service undertakings, was organized and successfully carried out in this spirit.

Hoover enjoyed his work as secretary of commerce and was pleased with the improvements his work had made. Under his leadership and with the input of handpicked experts, the once inefficient and ineffective department became a powerful force in the federal government. Over the years, Hoover had expanded the Commerce Department's reach by taking over bureaus from other departments.

As he had done in every place he worked, Hoover earned the respect and loyalty of many of the people who worked closely with him. "[H]e was a man of gentleness and consideration," remembered Bradley Nash, who worked under Hoover in the Department of Commerce. "He was awful thoughtful of me. He used to call me 'son' lots of times, and a shiver would run up my back, as he was a great hero to me."

While organizing, regulating, and advising the nation's businesses and industries, Secretary of Commerce Hoover did not overlook the nation's children. He served as president of the American Child Health Association and wrote the Child's Bill of Rights. "Our ideal is not only a child free from disease, it is also a child made free to develop to the utmost his capacity for physical, social and mental health," Hoover told members of the association in 1926.

In all that he did, Hoover followed the values of the Quaker faith, which included equality of all people in the eyes of God. In the last part of his term as secretary of commerce, Hoover desegregated a portion of the immense workforce under him and gave new opportunities to African Americans and women.

CHAPTER SIX

MR. PROSPERITY

*A chicken for every pot and a car
in every garage.*
—One of Hoover's campaign slogans
for the 1928 presidential election

Hoover was immensely popular with politicians and the public. Despite the Hoovers' objections, the public wanted to know more about the family, and newspapers were happy to oblige. One reporter, who described the Hoover home as "jovial, cheery, informal, folksy," went so far as to write about the foods the family enjoyed and the poor table manners of the Hoovers' dog Tut. Named for the Egyptian king Tutankhamen, whose ancient tomb had recently been discovered, Tut could always persuade his master to share bites under the breakfast table.

In 1927, when President Calvin Coolidge, a Republican, announced that he would not run for reelection, Republicans across the country began their own campaign.

One of Hoover's popular campaign slogans as it appeared in a 1928 issue of the New York Times *newspaper. The slogan accompanies a statement from Hoover on campaign issues.*

———————————— ✧

A Chicken *for* Every Pot

THE Republican Party isn't a *"Poor Man's Party."* Republican prosperity has erased that degrading phrase from our political vocabulary.

The Republican Party is *equality's* party—*opportunity's* party—*democracy's* party, the party of *national* development, not *sectional* interests—the *impartial* servant of every State and condition in the Union.

Under higher tariff and lower taxation, America has stabilized output, employment and dividend rates.

Republican efficiency has filled the workingman's dinner pail—and his gasoline tank *besides*—made telephone, radio and sanitary plumbing *standard* household equipment. And placed the whole nation in the *silk stocking class.*

During eight years of Republican management, we have built *more* and better homes, erected more skyscrapers, passed more beneficatory laws, and more laws to regulate and purify immigration, inaugurated more conservation measures, more measures to standardize and increase production, expand export markets, and reduce industrial and human junk piles, than in any previous quarter century.

Republican prosperity is written on *fuller* wage envelops, written in factory chimney smoke, written on the walls of new construction, written in savings bank books, written in mercantile balances, and written in the peak value of stocks and bonds.

Republican prosperity has *reduced* hours and *increased* earning capacity, silenced *discontent,* put the proverbial "chicken in every pot." And a car in every backyard, to boot.

It has *raised* living standards and *lowered* living costs.

It has restored financial confidence and enthusiasm, changed *credit* from a *rich* man's privilege to a *common*

utility, *generalized* the use of time-saving devices and released women from the thrall of *domestic drudgery.*

It has provided every county in the country with its concrete road and knitted the highways of the nation into a *unified* traffic system.

Thanks to Republican administration, farmer, dairyman and merchant can make deliveries in *less* time and at *less* expense, can borrow *cheap* money to re-fund exorbitant mortgages, and stock their pastures, ranges and shelves.

Democratic management *impoverished* and *demoralized* the *railroads,* led packing plants and tire factories into *receivership,* squandered billions on *impractical* programs.

Democratic mal-administration issued *further* billions on mere "scraps of paper," then encouraged foreign debtors to believe that their loans would never be called, and bequeathed to the Republican Party the job of *mopping up the mess.*

Republican administration has *restored* to the railroads solvency, efficiency and par securities.

It has brought the rubber trades through panic and chaos, brought down the prices of crude rubber by smashing *monopolistic rings,* put the tanner's books in the *black* and secured from the European powers formal acknowledgment of their obligations.

The Republican Party rests its case on a record of stewardship and performance.

Its Presidential and Congressional candidates stand for election on a platform of sound practice, Federal vigilance, high tariff, Constitutional integrity, the conservation of natural resources, *honest* and *constructive* measures for agricultural relief, sincere enforcement of the laws, and the right of *all* citizens, regardless of *faith* or *origin,* to share the benefits of opportunity and justice.

Wages, dividends, progress and prosperity say,

"Vote *for* Hoover"

An anonymous supporter paid for this full-page newspaper advertisement during the campaign.

They asked Hoover to run for president on the Republican ticket, with Charles Curtis as his running mate for vice president. Fifty-four-year-old Herbert Hoover accepted the nomination in Palo Alto, California, on August 11, 1928. Hoover was the first Quaker presidential candidate. His opponent, Democratic nominee Alfred E. Smith, was the nation's first Catholic presidential candidate. Al Smith was also a professional politician who had been governor of New York since 1923. Hoover had never run for public office, but the Great Humanitarian had a lot of public support.

For a man as shy and private as Hoover, campaigning for national office was difficult and uncomfortable. He made only seven public speeches during the campaign. Talking over the radio somewhat eased his fears, and for the first time, the radio played a major role in a presidential election. Hoover's popularity was great enough to make up for his quiet and reserved exterior.

With his belief in the superiority of all things from the United States, Hoover in many ways symbolized the prosperity that was sweeping the nation. His entrepreneurial spirit and confidence in new technology helped build his career and personal fortune. As a self-made man, he believed that the vision and dedication of individuals, cooperating

————————————— ✧ —————————————

Hoover supporters in California show their support for the presidential candidate in 1928. The poster of Hoover bears the campaign slogan, Who But Hoover?

Hoover speaks to a crowd about campaign issues from the back of a train car during the presidential campaign of 1928.

———————————— ✧ ————————————

with their fellow citizens, represented the road to prosperity and happiness and was the cure-all for misfortune.

One of Hoover's supporters was carmaker Henry Ford. He benefited tremendously from Hoover's standardization in industry and manufacturing. In endorsing Hoover, Ford said, "Mr. Hoover, it seems to me, is just the man we need today to clear the way for what I believe will be the greatest economic development the world has ever known."

THE ISSUES

Most people weren't worried about the U.S. economy in 1928, but other issues, such as prohibition and immigration, were a concern. In 1919 Congress passed prohibition—the ban on making, drinking, or distributing alcohol—making it the Eighteenth Amendment of the U.S. Constitution.

THE NEW ERA

The late 1920s were years of prosperity in the United States. After the war, people wanted to enjoy life again. The decade following the end of World War I in 1918 was known as the New Era. It was marked by increased spending and urban and industrial growth. More people lived in U.S. cities than in rural areas. Innovations in technology led to mass production and mass consumption of goods that made life easier and more fun. More and more people could purchase products such as washing machines, refrigerators, cars, and radios. Many people bought these items on credit and made payments. The 1920s also saw a boom in advertising. Manufacturers and retailers waged intense ad campaigns to entice the new middle class to buy products that once were only available to the rich.

During this decade of prosperity, Republican presidents, such as Harding and Coolidge, led the country. Republican leaders of the New Era supported big business and manufacturers in the United States with loans, new laws, and other benefits. Republicans believed that some degree of prosperity would eventually come to the ordinary citizen through the creation of jobs or an increase in wages.

During much of the 1920s, many people enjoyed prosperity and were able to buy expensive goods such as cars.

Many citizens believed that alcohol corrupted individuals and caused social problems such as violence, crime, and poverty. Business leaders believed that prohibition would prevent industrial accidents and promote better work habits in employees. Hoover was for prohibition while his opponent Alfred E. Smith supported its repeal.

In the 1920s, anti-immigrant sentiments were high. Between 1890 and 1920, almost nineteen million immigrants arrived in the United States. In 1921 the U.S. Congress passed legislation that dramatically restricted immigration into the country. Intolerance of foreigners, especially Catholic and Jewish immigrants, increased steadily as the decade progressed. Many people believed that if the president of the United States were Catholic, the pope (the leader of the Roman Catholic Church) would gain power over the country.

Smith was somewhat popular in the urban northern states, but he did not win the confidence of rural and small-town people. In the southern and midwestern states, most people were Protestants and supported prohibition. As a Quaker, Hoover believed in religious tolerance and freedom. He refused to use the nation's anti-Catholicism to his advantage in his presidential campaign, but many of his supporters raised the issue anyway.

PRESIDENT HOOVER

In November 1928, Hoover was elected the thirty-first president of the United States. He swept into the highest office in the land with an overwhelming majority of the vote—the largest in U.S. history to that time. Hoover had won forty of the country's forty-eight states.

President-elect Hoover (sitting back right) *arrives at his first stop in Central America in 1928. Hoover spoke with leaders about improving trade between the United States and Latin American countries.*

Almost immediately after the election, President-elect Hoover embarked on a six-week tour of Latin America. At the time, it was unusual for a U.S. president to travel abroad. After World War I, the United States had isolated itself from the rest of the world. The country restricted immigration and imposed tariffs, or taxes, on imported goods. Hoover hoped to improve strained relations and to encourage trade and commerce with Latin America.

The long trip was also an opportunity for Hoover to finalize plans for naming cabinet members and making other appointments. Between election and inauguration days, Hoover pulled together his staff and began to plan the goals and policies of his presidential administration.

By all appearances, the nation was happy, stable, and hopeful. After taking the oath of office on March 4, 1929, Hoover assured U.S. citizens, saying, "In no nation is the government more worthy of respect. No country is more loved by its people. I have an abiding faith in their capacity, integrity and high purpose. I have no fears for the future of our country. It is bright with hope."

CHAPTER SEVEN

THE PRESIDENCY

The mining world knew Hoover as the soundest . . . engineer in the business; the general public knew him not at all.

—Will Irwin, friend and biographer

Mornings in the Hoover White House began with a game of medicine ball on the lawn. Dubbed Hoover-ball by a reporter, the game involved tossing an eight-pound ball across a net. Hoover's staff, members of his cabinet, and other ranking officials all played the game. The morning routine was a model of efficiency—it provided exercise and, at the same time, an opportunity for Hoover to consult with his advisers.

Hoover applied this efficiency to his entire presidency. He was the first U.S. president to have a telephone on his office desk, eliminating the time required for face-to-face meetings. He also eliminated some presidential social traditions, including a daily greeting that required him to shake the hands of hundreds of White House visitors.

"The White House office was sorely afflicted with time-consuming and nerve-racking customs," Hoover wrote in his memoirs. "I learned that up to the beginning of the First World War the Presidents had spent only about two hours daily on office work. They spent another two or three hours a day seeing people and reporters."

Unfortunately, Hoover's attempt at efficiency worked against him. Fewer face-to-face meetings with ordinary citizens created more barriers between him and the public. People began to view Hoover as a distant president, out of touch with the needs of citizens.

BLACK TUESDAY

Only seven months into Hoover's presidency, the stock market crashed, or shut down. While the economy had appeared strong and stable, other forces were at work just under the surface, including speculation, or gambling, on the stock market. Many people borrowed money from banks to buy stocks or purchased stocks with little money down. These investors were confident that the stock's value would increase and that they could use the profits to pay back the money they owed. Banks began to buy stocks with their depositors' money, only to sell the stocks soon after to make a profit. All of this activity put the stock market at grave risk because it made the economy seem stronger than it actually was. In reality, industries were producing far more goods than consumers were buying or could afford to buy. When the market crashed on October 29, 1929 (known as Black Tuesday), stocks were suddenly worth a fraction of their original value, and investors lost billions of dollars.

Stock traders stand shocked on the floor of the New York Stock Exchange at the close of trading on Black Tuesday 1929. The stock market crashed on October 29, leaving many stocks worthless and investors penniless.

——————— ✧ ———————

When he was secretary of commerce, Hoover had been troubled by the stock market frenzy and the lack of laws to regulate the growing and risky transactions. He expressed this concern in reports and speeches as early as 1926. Almost immediately after taking office, President Hoover took steps to address the problem of stock speculating. He encouraged banks to impose self-regulation and asked newspapers and magazines to publish articles about the fragile state of the stock market. But few people listened.

Hoover, with his eye for large-scale problem solving, responded quickly to the stock market crash. He persuaded industry leaders to maintain wages and create new jobs by beginning necessary construction projects. Across the nation, state and federal public works projects were begun ahead of schedule, all in an attempt to steady the nation's wobbling economy. In the past, Hoover had used such voluntary cooperation with great success—from the food crisis in Belgium to the great flood of the Mississippi River. Like other economists of the time, Hoover believed that the economic slump caused by the crash was temporary. Nevertheless, Hoover also lowered taxes.

Other problems also existed in the economy before the crash. During World War I, farmers had enjoyed a great demand for their crops. As a result, they purchased land and additional equipment to expand their farms. When the wartime demand ended by 1920, farmers had produced more crops than people could buy, and the price of crops dropped. Hoover believed the government should help farmers figure out how to help each other. He did not believe that the government should regulate farm prices. Before the stock market crash, however, Hoover approved the Agricultural Marketing Act, which set up the Federal Farm Board to buy surpluses, raise grain prices, and provide farmers with agricultural loans.

SMOOT-HAWLEY TARIFF ACT

In 1930 Congress passed a new tariff on imported foreign goods in the form of the Smoot-Hawley bill. President Hoover did not veto the bill despite strong urgings from his advisers and foreign diplomats. He believed the bill would encourage consumers to buy more U.S. goods than foreign ones, which in turn would protect jobs and industry in the United States.

Despite the president's best intentions, the Smoot-Hawley Tariff Act actually made conditions worse instead of better.

Economic conditions in Europe had been deteriorating since World War I. With higher tariffs, European manufacturers lost a large foreign market for their goods. They responded by raising tariffs on U.S. goods, and the sale of these goods abroad dropped drastically.

In the United States, farmers needing to sell their crops were then left with fewer foreign markets. Crop prices fell sharply, and farmers found themselves unable to make payments on their land and equipment and unable to make a profit on their harvests.

European governments realized they could not repay the loans borrowed from the United States after World War I. The European economy began the same downward spiral as the United States, and entire financial structures crumbled.

CLASHING STYLES OF LEADERSHIP

Hoover's advisers, his political opponents, and other government leaders all urged him to approve direct assistance to the people. Hoover resisted this approach. He argued that handouts were an easy solution that would numb people of the need or desire to work. He vetoed any legislation proposing direct government assistance to individuals.

Hoover believed in what he called "indirect relief" as opposed to "direct relief." He thought the United States had the resources and determination to solve the problems of the Great Depression without government regulation. Hoover believed that it was the federal government's responsibility to help organizations such as businesses, manufacturers, large charities (such as the Red Cross), and local governments. These organizations would then benefit individuals and families in need. This belief was in keeping with the Republican

This cartoon plays on the story Gulliver's Travels. *It shows a disagreeing Congress* (the little people) *tying up Hoover and his efforts to solve the economic and social problems facing the United States.*

✧

economic philosophy of less, rather than more, interference from the federal government.

Hoover's Democratic opponents argued that people could not wait for government relief to make its way to their level. At the time, however, many Democrats—including Franklin Delano Roosevelt, who was then the governor of New York—also shared Hoover's objection to the federal government giving direct aid to the unemployed. Hoover and Roosevelt both believed that unemployment aid should come from state and local governments.

In 1930 the president founded the President's Emergency Committee for Employment to investigate unemployment. The committee suggested that the federal government approve $740 million for public works projects to create jobs and give financial relief to some of the five million unemployed in the United States. Hoover asked the U.S. Congress for a smaller sum, but lawmakers would only approve part of his request.

Throughout his presidency, Hoover was often frustrated with Congress, which was controlled by Democrats. Hoover was accustomed to having complete control over his work. The government's systems of checks and balances clashed with the president's work style, and the president clashed with the U.S. Congress.

THE GREAT DEPRESSION

In 1930 a severe drought in the southern and central United States intensified the already hard times. Farmers watched their crops wither and die in the fields and watched their topsoil blow away. The hardest hit states—Kansas, Colorado, Oklahoma, Texas, and New Mexico—would later be nick-named the Dust Bowl. The agricultural Dust Bowl made a bad situation worse for farmers and workers who were already struggling.

By the end of 1931, it became increasingly evident that the hard economic times that blanketed the nation were not temporary. Thousands of banks had closed, and many people had lost their life savings. Unemployment continued to rise, and people lost their homes. Homeless families erected shantytowns, or makeshift shacks on the outskirts of cities, living in hard and unsanitary conditions. As the Depression deepened, unemployment lines grew longer.

An understandably distraught and desperate public lashed out. Needing a scapegoat, or someone to blame for their struggles, the public targeted the president.

They showed their contempt for the president by nick-naming shantytowns Hoovervilles. Cars that were pulled by animals because there was not enough money to buy gas were called Hoovercarts. And people jokingly referred to empty pockets turned inside out as Hooverflags. Hoover's name became forever linked to the most severe economic crisis in the industrialized world.

With his unsmiling, no-nonsense exterior, Hoover was an easy target, and he did little to change public perception

────────────────── ✧ ──────────────────

A mother and daughter return to their home in a shantytown during the Great Depression. Those who blamed Hoover for the hardship of the economic depression often called shantytowns Hoovervilles.

CAMP RAPIDAN

To escape from the hectic schedule and grueling demands of the White House, the Hoovers built a rustic retreat and fishing camp called Camp Rapidan. The getaway was located in the Blue Ridge Mountains of Virginia, not far from Washington, D.C. The camp consisted of a cluster of log cabins that could accommodate about fifteen people at a time. Although the Hoovers paid for Camp Rapidan with their own money, they often used it as a place to conduct the work of the presidency and to entertain government officials and other leaders. When the Hoovers discovered that there was no school for children in the area, they used their own money to build one and to pay for a teacher. The Hoovers later donated Camp Rapidan to the National Park Service.

of him as a cold and unfeeling man. Only the people closest to him knew his true feelings and the depths of his compassion. "The scowl which he inherited from westerly ancestors means no more than an intense concentration of what to do next with a difficult problem or plan gone wrong," Hoover's brother Theodore once remarked.

Lou Henry Hoover tried to lift her husband's spirits by hosting dinner parties at the White House. The Hoovers used their own finances—which fared well despite the Great Depression—to throw these parties. But to the public, the parties were just another example of Hoover's heartlessness during the Depression.

While people accused Hoover of doing nothing and of not caring about their suffering, the president worked more than sixteen hours a day almost every day of his term.

During his presidency, stress and worry turned Hoover's hair white and caused him to lose twenty-five pounds. One reporter remembered that during the Great Depression, "I used to notice Mr. Hoover's eyes were bloodshot, as if he had gone sleepless during the night worrying about the problems that faced the nation."

Hoover eventually did approve direct government aid, not to individuals but to businesses. In 1932 he formed—and Congress approved—the Reconstruction Finance Corporation (RFC) to loan millions of dollars to failing businesses. The aid was slow to reach workers however, and unemployment increased.

THE BONUS ARMY

Following World War I, Congress had agreed that the U.S. government would pay each veteran of that war a certain sum of money in 1945 to compensate for wages lost during military service. Conditions were so bad that U.S. veterans asked for help. The veterans appealed to Congress to pay them early. When the government refused their request, veterans from across the country traveled to Washington, D.C., to sway the government with personal pleas and protests. In May 1932, almost twenty thousand veterans, nicknamed the Bonus Army, poured into the nation's capital and set up twenty-three separate barracks in abandoned buildings and parks.

After Congress reconsidered the bonus question and again decided against an early payout, most of the veterans returned home. Those who stayed continued to protest near the Capitol and the White House, taking over several abandoned government-owned buildings.

Hoover ordered them off government property. When they refused to budge, Hoover brought in the army to move the protesters back to their makeshift camp in Anacostia Park. As a Quaker, Hoover hated violence. Nevertheless, what happened next in the streets of Washington, D.C., would forever change the public's perception of Hoover's character.

Against the express orders of the president to use no more force than necessary, General Douglas MacArthur chased the veterans out of the city and ordered his soldiers to burn the veterans' camp. One thousand soldiers—some on horseback, some with machine guns—descended on the unarmed veterans, using undue force. Although under the

——————————— ✧ ———————————

The Bonus Army's camp burns in view of the U.S. Capitol Building.

command of General MacArthur, the soldiers were nevertheless acting against the orders of the president of the United States. When Hoover heard what MacArthur had done, he privately reprimanded the general. But in public, he allowed the press to blame him for the violence against the veterans.

Although he did not approve the veterans' request, Hoover had privately seen to their needs, even arranging for medical services to be made available in the camps. Phillips Brooks, a White House employee during the Hoover presidency, remembered how the Hoovers had helped the frustrated and exhausted protesters. "Mrs. Hoover used to have food prepared. . . to take out to the Bonus people," he said. "They were actually hungry. We would take trays of sandwiches and coffee." Throughout the Great Depression, the Hoovers quietly and anonymously spent thousands of dollars of their own money to help hundreds of needy people.

FDR AND THE NEW DEAL

In 1932 (an election year), unemployment had risen to an astonishing 25 percent of the U.S. workforce. People were scared, hungry, and desperate. The Republican Party again nominated Hoover as its presidential candidate, but few believed he would win against his charismatic and can-do opponent Franklin Roosevelt, the governor of New York. Like the rest of the nation, Roosevelt had watched and listened in horror to the stories of how the U.S. Army had attacked a group of defenseless veterans and burned their belongings. He is reported to have said, "This will elect me."

President Hoover (left) *accompanies President-elect Roosevelt on Inauguration Day in 1933. Placing much of the blame for the Great Depression on Hoover, voters chose to vote him out of office in 1932.*

Roosevelt was right. Hoover's failure to win reelection in November 1932 was a crushing political defeat. In a speech that October, Hoover had remarked that the campaign was "a contest between two philosophies of government." When the people voted, they decided it was time for a change and voiced their desire for Roosevelt's philosophy of government.

With his warmth, his cheerful smiles, and his easygoing manner, Roosevelt provided a welcome contrast to the dour and withdrawn Hoover. When Hoover avoided contact with the people and the press, Roosevelt sought it out. While Hoover campaigned with speeches stuffed with statistics and difficult economic terms, Roosevelt spoke of relieving the suffering of the people. And where Hoover was cautious, Roosevelt was bold, promising the public a "new deal."

In his first one hundred days as president, he worked with lawmakers to create fifteen major relief initiatives.

HOOVER'S PRESIDENTIAL LEGACY

Although Hoover's presidency is associated almost exclusively with the Great Depression, he made significant contributions to the nation during his four years in office. He helped bring about laws to protect young people and wrote a Children's Charter advocating their rights. He instituted regulations banning discrimination against women in the hiring practices of the federal government. He created the Veterans Administration to help those who had served in wars. He also initiated badly needed prison reforms and established the first ever Bureau of Prisons.

As a dedicated outdoorsman and naturalist, Hoover extended his caretaking efforts to the nation's forests, parks,

Hoover stands with his catch of the day. A naturalist, Hoover supported legislation during his presidency to protect parks and wildlife.

THE HOOVER DAM

During the Great Depression, disputes over water rights had exploded to near critical proportions in the southwestern United States. Seven states—Utah, Wyoming, Colorado, New Mexico, Arizona, California, and Nevada—depended on the unpredictable Colorado River for water. A dam proposed by Arthur Powell Davis in 1918 was scheduled to be built, but the states bitterly fought over how much water the dam would divert to each state. In 1922, as chairman of the Colorado River Commission, Hoover negotiated a resolution to the problem. He worked with the states to fairly divide the rights to the river.

Construction of the Hoover Dam began in 1931 about thirty miles southeast of Las Vegas, Nevada. The dam was one of the most ambitious and unprecedented engineering projects of its time. More than five thousand men worked for five years to complete the project. When completed, it stood 726 feet high and contained enough concrete to build a skyscraper taller than the Empire State Building.

After Hoover left office, the Roosevelt administration removed Hoover's name from the dam and renamed it Boulder Dam. When the project was dedicated in 1935, Hoover—who had paved the way for its construction—was not even invited to the dedication ceremony. This was a huge blow to him. (President Harry S. Truman changed the name back to Hoover Dam in 1947.)

Hoover Dam construction

and wildlife. He protected many species of birds and other wildlife by greatly increasing the amount of land conserved in national parks and by placing restrictions on oil drilling and hunting. He also proposed the construction of several dams in the western United States to give flood protection and create jobs.

One of these dams, the Hoover Dam, was the most ambitious project of its kind. When finished it was the world's largest dam. During Hoover's four years in office, the federal government spent more money on public works projects, such as the dam construction, than it had spent in the previous thirty years.

It would take decades before history revealed that much of Hoover's work contributed to President Roosevelt's achievements. "We didn't admit it at the time," a Roosevelt adviser said in 1974, "but practically the whole New Deal was extrapolated from programs that Hoover started."

Hoover's good works, however, were overshadowed by the raw reality of unemployment lines, soup kitchens, and the hungry. In four years, he had almost completely lost the affection, respect, and confidence of the United States. While the citizens of Europe celebrated Hoover as a hero and named schools and streets after him, to a generation of people in the United States he would forever symbolize heartache and hardship. By the end of his four-year term, Hoover was tired, frustrated, and hurt. "Why is it," he once asked an aide, "that when a man is on the job as I am day and night, doing the best he can, that certain men . . . seek to oppose everything he does, just to oppose him?"

CHAPTER EIGHT

ELDER STATESMAN

Being a politician is a poor profession.
Being a public servant is a noble one.
—Herbert Hoover, in a letter to an American child

Lou and Herbert Hoover left the White House in March 1933 and returned home to Palo Alto, California. They also spent time in New York. Presidents and their family were usually given Secret Service protection after leaving the White House, but the Hoovers were deprived of it. When the commissioner of the New York City Police Department learned of this, he was appalled. He assigned plainclothes officers to guard Hoover. At the sight of these men, people began to spread ugly rumors that the government had hired the officers to watch Hoover so he would not escape with a fortune in gold. Others believed that the Hoovers sailed away in a luxury yacht, loaded down with gold stolen from the nation.

Many of these rumors had been intentionally started and spread by the Democratic Party. In a deliberate smear cam-

President Hoover with his family in the early 1930s. (From left to right)
Allan Hoover, Margaret Hoover (wife of Herbert Hoover Jr.),
Herbert Hoover Jr., Lou Hoover, and Hoover.

paign, the Democrats had hired a publicity expert for the sole purpose of spreading bad—and usually false—news about the Hoovers. The former president was deeply hurt by these ridiculous and slanderous stories and by the disrespectful treatment he received from the Roosevelt administration.

Immediately upon losing the election in 1932, Hoover had sent a telegram to Roosevelt congratulating the president-elect and offering his service to him and the nation. "In the common purpose of all of us I shall dedicate myself to every possible helpful effort," Hoover wrote.

The following day, the *New York Times* reported that Roosevelt "preferred not to make reply or comment on the message."

Thus began Hoover's twelve-year exile from U.S. government and politics. Hoover disliked Roosevelt and strongly opposed his New Deal programs, which Hoover thought gave the president and federal government too much power. It wasn't until after President Roosevelt's death that Hoover was welcomed back to the White House. The slight was felt deeply by Hoover. "Above all, Mr. Hoover wanted to be useful," remembered a *Washington Post* reporter who sometimes traveled with the Hoovers.

It was not easy for the former president to be the man despised by a nation and slighted by the new president of the United States. Lou compared her husband's effort to weather the storm of criticism and slander to someone trying to recover from a long and painful illness. In the first months after leaving office, Hoover stayed close to his Palo Alto home, a lovely modern house Lou had designed and built near the campus of Stanford University. His son Allan accompanied him on a fishing trip in hopes of raising his spirits. "You are the last of cheerful companionship," Lou told her son. "He has had a long, dull, deadly grind . . . and he needs bright spots."

Years later, a reporter, reflected back upon the years following Hoover's 1932 defeat. He wrote, "Herbert Hoover has quietly continued to conduct himself as a gentleman."

OUTSIDE OF POLITICS

Dividing his time between California and New York, Hoover gave speeches, wrote articles and books, and raised money for Stanford University, which always remained dear to his heart. When the Boys Clubs of America invited him to join its board in 1936 and elected him chairman, Hoover began a fulfilling and meaningful relationship with the organization, one that would last for more than a quarter of a century. Throughout a lifetime of public service to the world, helping children had remained a huge priority. Under his leadership, the organization added five hundred new clubs.

In 1939 Germany invaded Poland, and World War II began. As the United States itself moved closer to war, Polish government leaders, who had been exiled by the German invaders, asked Hoover to coordinate relief efforts for Polish citizens. For two years, Hoover and his privately established Polish Relief Commission fed about 300,000 Polish children.

One newspaper editorial praised Hoover's latest efforts and declared in October 1941, "[Herbert Hoover] has moved straight forward, refusing to give up his struggle to carry mercy and pity and friendship to the most hopeless victims of war. We believe that he is only now approaching the summit of his career."

LIFE WITHOUT LOU

In December 1941, the Japanese attacked Pearl Harbor, on the island of Oahu, Hawaii, and the United States entered World War II. Hoover spent most of the war years writing his memoirs. During this period, he also lost his lifelong companion and intellectual partner, Lou, who died on January 7, 1944. Only sixty-nine years old, she had suffered a heart attack while napping in the Hoover's Waldorf-Astoria apartment in New York City.

LOU HENRY HOOVER

The daughter of a banker and a schoolteacher, Lou Henry was born in Waterloo, Iowa, in 1874—the same year as her husband and just sixty miles from his West Branch birthplace.

Lou's father, Charles Henry, taught her to love nature and enjoy the outdoors. From the time she could walk, Lou accompanied her father on hiking, fishing, and camping trips. Lou learned how to hunt and fish and how to identify rocks, flowers, wildlife, and trees. She learned horseback riding on her uncle's farm and became an expert horsewoman.

When Lou was eleven, her parents moved the family, which included a younger sister, Jean, to California. The Henrys believed that the milder climate would be good for Mrs. Henry's poor health.

As she grew, Lou learned the value of hard work and service to others. In school, sports, and clubs, she demonstrated clear leadership qualities and a spirit of teamwork.

After high school, Lou attended a teacher's college and studied education. She became fascinated with geology after attending a lecture by a famous geologist teaching at Stanford University. Determined to become a geologist, Lou enrolled at Stanford and became the first female student in the geology and mines department. Her decision to further her education was life changing.

In a geology lab at Stanford, she met her future husband, Herbert Hoover. The two were married after Lou had completed her studies and Hoover had begun his engineering career.

During their marriage, the Hoovers circled the globe many times, and Lou made a comfortable home for her growing family wherever she went. Her relaxed social graces and her knack for languages made her a warm and inviting hostess. She often assisted her husband on numerous mining and geological projects.

Lou is probably best remembered for her lifelong commitment to public service. Wherever she went, she found a way to help others. In 1914, while her husband was aiding stranded U.S. citizens with their financial and transportation problems in London, Lou organized a project to help women and children from the United States. She arranged places for them to stay and collected food and clothing.

Lou Henry Hoover

While her husband was serving the nation as the U.S. food administrator, Lou became involved with the Girl Scouts. She first served as a troop leader but went on to hold various leadership positions throughout the national organization. She remained devoted to the Girl Scouts for the rest of her life.

During the Great Depression, she anonymously helped all sorts of people who were left destitute and homeless by the financial crisis. In Virginia, near the Hoovers' Camp Rapidan retreat, Lou even financed and oversaw the building of a school for local children.

As First Lady, she also initiated, at her own expense, various renovation and restoration projects in the White House. In 1935 she purchased her husband's tiny birthplace cottage in West Branch, Iowa, and restored the structure to its 1874 appearance.

A lifelong advocate of sports and exercise for girls, Lou never lost her love of the outdoors. Lou Henry Hoover died of a heart attack on January 7, 1944, at the age of sixty-nine.

While looking through his wife's papers after her death, Hoover found an emotional letter written to their sons. "You have been lucky boys to have had such a father," Lou had written, "and I am a lucky woman to have had my life trail alongside the lives of three such men. . . . " Hoover also came across uncashed checks that totaled in the tens of thousands of dollars. Throughout her lifetime, Lou had loaned money to people in need. These were the checks to repay the loans. She never cashed them.

A FRIEND IN TRUMAN

With the death of President Roosevelt in April 1945, Hoover's long exile from the political scene was lifted. The new president, Harry S. Truman, invited Hoover to the White House the month after Roosevelt's death. Truman knew Hoover by reputation only but was certain the nation could use his skills and talents.

———————————————— ✦ ————————————————

President Hoover (right) meets with President Harry S. Truman in 1946. Hoover was an adviser and a friend to Truman.

World War II had just ended in Europe, and Truman asked Hoover to investigate the food status there. At seventy years old, Hoover worked tirelessly for the millions of people still suffering in the aftermath of war. He traveled more than fifty thousand miles in three months and met with leaders of more than forty countries. Upon his return to the United States, he made recommendations to reduce U.S. food consumption and aid war-torn countries. He then left to do similar relief work in Latin America.

Although aligned with different political parties, Truman the Democrat and Hoover the Republican formed a strong friendship that was as much personal as it was political. "Yours has been a friendship which has reached deeper into my life than you know," Hoover once told Truman.

THE HOOVER COMMISSION

In 1947 President Truman and the U.S. Congress asked Hoover to head a commission that would report on the organization of the executive branch of the federal government.

Hoover and the first Hoover Commission found that the federal government had grown much too large after two world wars. The commission made many recommendations—from creating new cabinet positions for a secretary of health and a secretary of defense to reorganizing the government's budget. More than 70 percent of the commission's recommendations for eliminating governmental waste and for maximizing efficiency, service, and productivity were implemented and remain in effect. It is estimated that Hoover's recommendations save the federal government and U.S. taxpayers three billion dollars a year.

Members of the first Hoover Commission remembered that Hoover did not miss a single meeting in the two years of its existence. His colleagues were impressed by his ability to digest huge portions of information and to distill details down to short, efficient reports and recommendations.

In 1953, following the Korean War, President Dwight D. Eisenhower asked Hoover to head a similar commission concerning the responsibilities of the federal government. Almost eighty years old, Hoover worked tirelessly for two years and accepted no payment for his work.

During the second Hoover Commission, the U.S. Congress passed its first unanimous resolution of thanks to one person. In June 1954, the congressional body that Hoover had sparred with so vehemently during his presidency thanked him for his "devoted service to his country and to the world."

THE GREAT HUMANITARIAN REMEMBERED

In his eighties, Hoover had no intention of slowing down and still put in eight to twelve hours of work a day. In his residential suite in the Waldorf-Astoria Hotel in New York City, Hoover kept an office and employed a staff of secretaries. Although his apartment lifestyle did not permit the large menagerie of pets so customary for the Hoover household, Hoover did enjoy the company of Mr. Cat, his pet Siamese cat. Hoover continued to travel and was honored frequently with citations and invitations to speak at various functions. When he had the time, he visited the Florida Keys for fishing holidays with his sons and grandchildren.

The elder statesman still received a tremendous amount of mail and insisted that each letter receive a personal

A smiling Herbert Hoover in 1954. In that year, the president received congressional thanks for his service to the nation and to the world.

———————————— ✧ ————————————

response. "Even those without addresses we would spend time and try to find out how we could acknowledge them because this is what Mr. Hoover wanted," remembered one of his secretaries. "You wanted to do your very best for him. . . . He brought out the best in anyone."

Hoover particularly enjoyed his correspondence with children, who wrote to him by the thousands from all over the world. "Answering their letters . . . has been a great relief from the haunts of nights sleepless with public anxiety," Hoover said. In 1962 the former president published some of these letters in a book, *On Growing Up: Letters to American Boys and Girls.*

On August 10, 1962, his eighty-eighth birthday, Hoover returned to his West Branch birthplace for the dedication of the Herbert Hoover Presidential Library. He asked his old friend, former president Harry S. Truman, to be his special guest at the ceremony.

In the following two years, Hoover's health gradually declined. News of his failing health spread quickly, and get-well wishes came from around the world—from family and friends, from diplomats and politicians, and from ordinary people.

But after more than fifty years of service to the nation and the world, Herbert Hoover died at his home in New

More than seventy thousand leaders, dignitaries, and citizens attended
President Hoover's funeral (above) on October 25, 1964.

York City on October 20, 1964, with his family and friends at his bedside. He was ninety years old. "I knew I had witnessed the death of just about the finest man I had ever known," remembered Hoover's doctor and close friend Michael J. LePore.

At the news of Hoover's death, President Lyndon Johnson ordered flags to be lowered to half-mast. The chief justice of the U.S. Supreme Court ordered an immediate recess of the court's proceedings. On the Stanford University campus, the bells in the Hoover Tower tolled in tribute to the country's thirty-first president. And across the nation, members of the Boys Clubs of America mourned the loss of their leader and sent hundreds of telegrams to the Hoover family. Kings, presidents, governors, and others also flooded the Hoover family with condolences. The president of Finland said his country would "cherish [Hoover's] memory as the most warm-hearted statesman this century has brought forth."

On October 25, 1964, Herbert Hoover was buried in West Branch, Iowa. More than seventy thousand people attended the simple graveside ceremony to pay their respects to the Great Humanitarian.

TIMELINE

1874   Herbert Clark Hoover is born in West Branch, Iowa, on August 10.

1880   Hoover's father, Jesse Hoover, dies.

1884   Hoover's mother, Hulda Minthorn Hoover, dies.

1885   Eleven-year-old Hoover moves to Newberg, Oregon, to live with relatives.

1889–1891   Hoover works for his uncle's land company and takes business classes at night.

1891   Seventeen-year-old Hoover enrolls at Stanford University.

1894   Hoover meets Lou Henry at Stanford University.

1895   Hoover graduates from Stanford University with a geology degree.

1896   Hoover works in a California mine as a laborer and later as a mining engineer for Louis Janin.

1897–1899   Hoover works as a mining engineer in London and Australia for the firm of Bewick, Moreing and Company.

1899   Hoover returns to California to marry Lou Henry on February 10.

1899–1901   Hoover works in China as a mining engineer.

1900   Herbert and Lou Henry Hoover help ward off rebelling Chinese peasants in the Boxer uprising.

1903   Herbert Clark Hoover Jr. is born.

1907   Allan Henry Hoover is born.

1908 The Hoover family moves back to the United States. Hoover starts his own mining firm.

1912 Herbert and Lou Henry Hoover publish a translation of *De Re Metallica,* an important sixteenth-century mining document. Stanford University elects Hoover to its board of trustees.

1914 Herbert and Lou assist thousands of stranded U.S. tourists in London, England.

1914–1917 Hoover directs the Commission for Relief in Belgium and other relief programs in Europe.

1917–1919 President Woodrow Wilson appoints Hoover U.S. food administrator.

1919 Hoover creates the Hoover Institution on War, Revolution and Peace at Stanford.

1921–1928 Hoover serves as secretary of commerce under presidents Harding and Coolidge.

1922 The people of Belgium honor Hoover with a bronze statue of Isis, the Egyptian goddess of life.

1928 Hoover is elected the thirty-first president of the United States.

1929 The Agricultural Marketing Act is passed to aid farmers. The stock market crashes on October 29, and the Great Depression is set in motion.

1930 Congress passes and Hoover approves the Smoot-Hawley Tariff Act, which raises tariffs on foreign imports. President Hoover's Emergency Committee for Employment is established to find solutions to the unemployment problems created by the Great Depression.

1931 Construction begins on the Hoover Dam.

1932 The Reconstruction Finance Corporation (RFC) is created to give loans to failing businesses and banks. General Douglas MacArthur forces the Bonus Army, a group of World War I veterans, to leave Washington, D.C. Franklin Delano Roosevelt is elected president.

1933 The Hoovers return home to California.

1934 The Hoovers divide their time between California and New York City.

1936 Hoover is elected chairman of the Boys Clubs of America.

1944 Lou Henry Hoover dies.

1945 President Harry Truman appoints Hoover to investigate the food crisis in Europe following World War II.

1947 Hoover heads the first Hoover Commission.

1953 Hoover heads the second Hoover Commission.

1954 The U.S. Congress passes its first ever unanimous resolution of thanks, in appreciation of Hoover's public service.

1962 The Herbert Hoover Presidential Library opens in West Branch, Iowa.

1964 Herbert Hoover dies on October 20 at the age of ninety.

Source Notes

7 Eugene Lyons, *The Herbert Hoover Story* (Washington, DC: Human Events, 1959), 19.

7 James P. Johnson, "Herbert Hoover: The Orphan as Children's Friend," *Children's Bureau,* Winter 1980, 201.

8 Ibid.

9 Republican National Committee, *Herbert Hoover Returns to Boyhood Scenes,* (Washington, DC: Republican National Committee, 1928), 3.

9 Amy Ruth, "Herbie the Presidential Cat" (picture book manuscript, unpublished, Herbert Hoover Presidential Library, 1997), 2.

12 Herbert Hoover, *Years of Adventure, 1874–1920,* vol. 1, *The Memoirs of Herbert Hoover* (New York: Macmillan, 1952), 3.

14 Ibid., 8.

15 Ibid., 10.

15 Ibid., 11.

15 Burt Brown Barker, oral history interview by Raymond Henle, October 17, 1967, transcript, Herbert Hoover Presidential Library, West Branch, IA, 17.

15 Hoover, *Years of Adventure,* 11.

16 Barker, oral history interview, 17.

16 Hoover, *Years of Adventure,* 13.

16 "Thank You Miss Gray!" *Readers Digest,* n.d., 119.

19 Hoover, *Years of Adventure,* 15.

20 David Burner, *Herbert Hoover: A Public Life* (New York: Alfred A. Knopf, 1979), 27.

22 Hoover, *Years of Adventure,* 17.

22 John C. Branner, "Herbert Hoover as an Educational Illustration," John Casper Branner Papers, 1882–1921. Alumni of Stanford University, San Francisco, December 29, 1919, 2.

22 Will Irwin, *Herbert Hoover: A Reminiscent Biography* (New York: Century, 1928), 48.

22 Hoover, *Years of Adventure,* 20.

23 George H. Nash, *The Engineer, 1874–1914,* vol. 1, *The Life of Herbert Hoover* (New York: W. W. Norton, 1983), 35.

24 Irwin, *Herbert Hoover: A Reminiscent Biography,* 54.

24 John Garrity, "Which of These Men Is the Real Herbert Hoover?" *Smithsonian,* May 1985, 146.

26 Hoover, *Years of Adventure,* 23.

27 Ibid.

27 Ibid., 26.

30 Herbert Hoover, quoted in Richard Norton Smith, *An Uncommon Man: The Triumph of Herbert Hoover* (New York: Simon and Schuster, 1984), 67.

31 Barker, oral history interview, 34–35.

33 Burner, *Herbert Hoover: A Public Life,* 28.

33 Hoover, *Years of Adventure,* 33.

33 Ibid., 38.

34 Ibid., 36.

35 Ibid., 40.

38 Ibid., 50.

40 Hoover, *Years of Adventure,* 148.

40 "Hoover Online: Highest Salaried Man of His Age in the World," *Hoover Museum-Digital Archives,* June 20, 2001, <http://www.ecommcode.com/hoover/hooveronline/hoover_bio/archive/china/high.htm> (November 2003).

42 Herbert Hoover, speech at opening session of White House Conference on Child Health and Protection, Washington, DC, November 19, 1930.

42 William Hard, "Friend Hoover," *The Christian Herald,* September 1928, 952.

44 Lou Hoover to Herbert Hoover, telegram, May 1914, Herbert Hoover Presidential Library, West Branch, IA.

44 Lou Hoover to Herbert Hoover, telegram, June 11, 1914, Herbert Hoover Presidential Library, West Branch, IA.

44 Lyons, *The Herbert Hoover Story,* 132.

46 Hoover, *Years of Adventure,* 148.

48 Ibid., 155.

49 Ibid., 178.

50 Robertson Smith, "Hoover the Man in Action," unpublished manuscript, n.d., Herbert Hoover Presidential Library, West Branch, IA, 4.

51 Ibid.

52 "Hoover Online: World War I," *Hoover Museum-Digital Archives,* June 20, 2001, <http://www.ecommcode.com/ hoover/ hooveronline/hoover_bio/wwi.htm> (November 4, 2003).

53 Branner, "Herbert Hoover as an Educational Illustration," 5.

54 Herbert Hoover, "Address at the Annual Dinner of the Chamber of Commerce of the United States" (Washington, DC: GPO, 1930).

54 "Hoover Online: U.S. Food Administrator," *Hoover Museum-Digital Archives,* June 20, 2001, <http://www. ecommcode.com/ hoover/hooveronline/hoover_bio/food. htm> (November 5, 2003).

55 Herbert Hoover, "Why I Ask Your Help," *Ladies Home Journal,* October 1917, 18.

58 Joan Hoff Wilson, *Herbert Hoover: Forgotten Progressive* (Prospect Heights, IL: Waveland Press, Inc., 1992), 79.

60 Herbert Hoover, *American Individualism* (1922; reprint, West Branch, IA: Herbert Hoover Presidential Library Association, 1997), 6.

63 Bradley D. Nash, oral history interview by Raymond Henle, July 31, 1968, transcript, Herbert Hoover Presidential Library, West Branch, IA, 69.

63 Herbert Hoover, speech, Annual Meeting of the American Child Health Association, Atlantic City, May 18, 1926, Herbert Hoover Presidential Library, West Branch, Iowa.

64 Hoover's 1928 campaign slogan.

64 Allene Sumner, "Strawberries, Hound, and Mrs. Hoover Present When Mr.Hoover Breakfasts," *New York Telegram,* May 23, 1928, Herbert Hoover Presidential Library, West Branch, IA.

67 Republican National Committee, *Henry Ford Tells Why He's for Hoover,* (Washington, DC: RNC, 1928), 5.

68 "History of the United States: War, Prosperity and the Big Crash (1900s to 1929)," *U.S. Diplomatic Mission to Germany/Public Affairs/Information Resource Centers, June 2003,* <http://www.usembassy.de/usa/ history-ww1.htm> (September 13, 2003).

71 Herbert Hoover, "Inaugural Address of Herbert Hoover, President of the United States" Washington, D.C., March 4, 1929" (Washington, DC: GPO, 1929), 11.

72 Irwin, *Herbert Hoover: A Reminiscent Biography,* 39.

73 Herbert Hoover, *The Cabinet and the Presidency, 1920–1933,* vol. 2, *The Memoirs of Herbert Hoover* (New York: Macmillan, 1952), 325–326.

80 Louise Hoover Stevenson, oral history interview by Raymond Henle, January 1970, transcript, Herbert Hoover Presidential Library, West Branch, IA, 13.

81 Edward T. Folliard, oral history interview by Raymond Henle, August 6, 1968, transcript, Herbert Hoover Presidential Library, West Branch, IA, 4–5.

83 PhillipsP. Brooks, oral history interview by Raymond Henle, September 1, 1970, transcript, Herbert Hoover Presidential Library, West Branch, IA, 12–13.

83 Burner, *Herbert Hoover: A Public Life,* 311.

84 Herbert Hoover, Address at Madison Square Garden, New York City, October 31, 1932.

87 Burner, *Herbert Hoover: A Public Life,* 244.

87 Wilson, *Herbert Hoover: Forgotten Progressive,* 147.

88 Herbert Hoover, *On Growing Up: Letters to American Boys and Girls,* ed. William Nichols (New York: William Morrow, 1962), 36.

89 "The President's Message to the President-Elect," *New York Times,* November 9, 1932, 1.

90 Ibid.

90 Folliard, oral history interview, 17.

90 Dale C. Mayer, ed., *Lou Henry Hoover: Essays on a Busy Life* (Worland, WY.: High Plains Publishing, 1994), 116.

90 Russ Hyatt, "The Hoover Smear Was Dirty Politics at Its Very Dirtiest," *Wichita Kansas Beacon,* August 19, 1959.

91 Lyons, *The Herbert Hoover Story,* 334.

94 Draft article for *This Week* magazine, June 1954, Herbert Hoover Presidential Library, West Branch, IA, 11.

95 "Gallery Nine: Counselor to the Republic," *The Museum Exhibit Galleries,* August 29, 2001, <http://www.hoover.archives.gov/exhibits/Hooverstory/gallery09/gallery09.html> (November 4, 2003).

96 *This Week,* 11.

97 M. Elizabeth Dempsey, oral history interview by Raymond Henle, July 13, 1967, transcript, Herbert Hoover Presidential Library, West Branch, IA, 36.

97 "Children Melted Hoover's Shyness," *New York Times,* October 21, 1964, 41.

99 Michael J. LePore, M.D., oral history interview by Raymond Henle, December 5, 1966, transcript, Herbert Hoover Presidential Library, West Branch, Iowa, 30.

99 "Johnson, Eisenhower and Truman Lead the Nation in Tributes to Herbert Hoover," *New York Times,* October 21, 1964, 41.

Selected Bibliography

Branner, John C. "Herbert Hoover as an Educational Illustration." John Casper Branner Papers, 1882–1921. Unpublished paper, Alumni of Stanford University, San Francisco, December 29, 1919.

Burner, David. *Herbert Hoover: A Public Life.* New York: Alfred A. Knopf, 1979.

"Herbert Hoover Presidential Library and Museum: The Herbert Hoover Galleries." *The Museum Exhibit Galleries..* August 29, 2001. <http://www.hoover.archives.gov/exhibits/Hooverstory/> (November 4, 2003).

"Herbert Hoover Presidential Library and Museum: Hoover Online Digital Archives," *Hoover Museum-Digital Archives.* June 20, 2001. <http://www.ecommcode.com/hoover/hooveronline/> (November 4, 2003).

"History of the United States: War, Prosperity and the Big Crash (1900s to 1929)." *U.S. Diplomatic Mission to Germany/Public Affairs/ Information Resource Centers.* June 2003. <http://www.usembassy.de/ usa/history-ww1.htm> (September 13, 2003).

Hoover family. Papers. Herbert Hoover Presidential Library, West Branch, IA.

Hoover, Herbert. *American Individualism.* 1922. West Branch, IA: Herbert Hoover Presidential Library Association, 1997.

———. *The Memoirs of Herbert Hoover.* 3 vols. New York: Macmillan, 1951–1952.

———. *On Growing Up: Letters to American Boys and Girls.* Edited by William Nichols. New York: William Morrow and Company, 1962.

Hoover, Lou. Papers. Personal correspondence, 1872–1920. Herbert Hoover Presidential Library, West Branch, IA.

Irwin, Will. *Herbert Hoover: A Reminiscent Biography.* New York: Century, 1928.

Lyons, Eugene. *The Herbert Hoover Story.* Washington, DC: Human Events, 1959.

Mayer, Dale C., ed. *Lou Henry Hoover: Essays on a Busy Life.* Worland, WY: High Plains Publishing, 1994.

Nash, George H. *The Life of Herbert Hoover.* 3 vols. New York: W. W. Norton, 1966–1988.

New York Times, October 21, 1964, 41.

Oral history interviews by Raymond Henle. Tape recording. 1966–1970. Herbert Hoover Presidential Library, West Branch, IA.

Ruth, Amy. "Herbie the Presidential Cat." Picture book manuscript, Herbert Hoover Presidential Library, 1997.

Smith, Gene. *The Shattered Dream: Herbert Hoover and the Great Depression.* New York: William Morrow, 1970.

Smith, Richard Norton. *An Uncommon Man: The Triumph of Herbert Hoover.* New York: Simon and Schuster, 1984.

Wilson, Joan Hoff. *Herbert Hoover: Forgotten Progressive.* Prospect Heights, IL: Waveland Press, Inc., 1992.

FURTHER READING AND WEBSITES

Blumenthal, Karen. *Six Days in October: The Stock Market Crash of 1929.* New York: Atheneum Books for Young Readers, 2002.

Damon, Duane. *Headin' for Better Times: The Arts of the Great Depression.* Minneapolis: Lerner Publications Company, 2001.

DuTemple, Leslie A. *The Hoover Dam.* Minneapolis: Lerner Publications Company, 2003.

Faber, Doris. *The Smithsonian Book of the First Ladies: Their Lives, Times, and Issues.* Edited by Edith P. Mayo. With a foreword by Hillary Rodham Clinton. New York: Smithsonian Institution Press, 1996.

Farrell, Jacqueline. *The Great Depression.* San Diego: Lucent Books, 1996.

Feinberg, Barbara Silberdick. *Black Tuesday: The Stock Market Crash of 1929.* Brookfield, CT: Millbrook Press, 1995.

Feldman, Ruth Tenzer. *World War I.* Minneapolis: Lerner Publications Company, 2004.

Nardo, Don. *The Great Depression.* San Diego: Greenhaven Press, 1998.

Nash, George H. *The Life of Herbert Hoover.* 3 vols. New York: W. W. Norton, 1983–96.

Nishi, Dennis. *Life during the Great Depression.* San Diego: Lucent Books, 1998.

Ray, Delia. *Ghost Girl: A Blue Ridge Mountain Story.* New York: Clarion, 2003.

Rensberger, Susan. *A Multicultural Portrait of the Great Depression.* Tarrytown, NY: Benchmark Books, 1996.

Roberts, Jeremy. *Franklin D. Roosevelt.* Minneapolis: Lerner Publications Company, 2003.

Robinson, Edgar Eugene, and Vaughn D. Bornet. *Herbert Hoover: President of the United States.* Hoover Institution Press, 1975.

Ruth, Amy. *Growing Up in the Great Depression, 1929 to 1941.*
Minneapolis: Lerner Publications Company, 2003.

Turkel, Studs. *Hard Times: An Oral History of the Great Depression.*
New York: New Press/W. W. Norton, 2000.

Williams, Jean Kinney. *The Quakers.* New York: Franklin Watts,
1998.

WEBSITES

The Herbert Hoover Presidential Library-Museum.
<http://hoover.archives.gov/>. This official website of the Hoover
Library provides extensive information about Hoover's private life
and public service. Visitors can take a tour of the museum's virtual
galleries or use the on-line digital archives to view some of the
thousands of primary materials housed in the library and museum.

"Hoover Dam." *The American Experience.*
<http://www.pbs.org/wgbh/amex/hoover/index.html>. A guide to
PBS's documentary on the Hoover Dam. The website includes an
enhanced transcript of the program, a timeline, maps, and further
information about the people and events of the dam's construction.

Hoover Dam: A National Historic Landmark.
<http://www.usbr.gov/lc/hooverdam/index.html>. This official
website of the Hoover Dam is maintained by the U.S. Bureau of
Reclamation. Visitors can learn more about the history and current
use of the dam.

"Lou Henry Hoover." *The White House.*
<http://www.whitehouse.gov/history/firstladies/lh31.html>. This is
the White House's biography of the former First Lady.

INDEX

ABOUT THE AUTHOR

Amy Ruth is the author of *Growing Up in the Great Depression, 1929 to 1941* and several biographies for young readers, including *Mother Teresa, Louisa May Alcott, Jane Austen,* and *Queen Latifah.* She lives in Williamsburg, Virginia.

✦

PHOTO ACKNOWLEDGMENTS

The images in this book are used with the permission of: courtesy of the Library of Congress, pp. 2 [LC-USZ62-33277], 6 [LC-USZ62-094862], 21 [LC-USZ62-096641], 36 [LC-USZ62-112326], 50 [LC-USZ62-112615], 59 [LC-USZ62-111712], 67 [LC-USZ62-102518], 70 [LC-USZ62-106386], 79 [LC-USF34-9995C], 84 [LC-USA7-18241], 93 [LC-USZ62-25811], 94 [LC-USZ62-076325], 97 [LC-USZ62-116547]; courtesy of the White House, pp. 1, 7, 9, 20, 30, 40, 54, 64, 72, 88; © Brown Brothers, pp. 10, 56, 66, 89; courtesy of the Herbert Hoover Presidential Library, pp. 11, 13, 18, 23, 25, 26, 28, 31, 32, 37, 41, 42, 45, 47, 55, 60, 65, 74, 98; © CORBIS, p. 34; National Archives, pp. 52 [W&C 428], 82 [NWDNS-111-SC-97532], 85 [NWDNS-22-N-8960]; National Archives Rocky Mountain Region, p. 86 [NRG-115-CONSTPHO85006-BC21442]; © Hulton| Archive by Getty Images, p. 57; © Swim Ink/CORBIS, p. 68; © J. N. "Ding" Darling Foundation, p. 77.

Cover photo: courtesy of the Library of Congress [LC-USZ62-24155]